HOW TO WIN & KEEP CLIENTS

ISBN: 978-1-5272-4613-3

First published: 2019

Dedication

This book is dedicated to every person who has tried and succeeded, or tried and failed, to run a successful business. It is dedicated to everyone who wants to make a difference to the lives of others, to all those we have learned from, and to those who still have so much to teach.

It is also dedicated to you, dear reader, for no other reason, perhaps, than your desire to create a legacy and do something that will benefit others. And for that, you are to be commended.

Foreword

By

Leon Taylor

I was attracted to supporting this important and unique self-help business book, because I'm in the midst of my own business adventure after a life of sport – so this book totally resonated with me. Having competed at the highest level for over 16 years, I was a little lost as I moved into my next career. One of the best ways to excel in any area is to find people who are already making headway, and learn directly from them. This book allows you to do just that. It's a playbook for success – but only if you commit and are willing to put the work in.

The lessons in this book are perfect for anyone looking to establish their dream business, increase their clients and their income, and start loving the life they live – both professionally and personally. By proactively applying the strategies laid out in this book, in the right way, I guarantee that you will get the utmost value from the incredible team of authors – and enhance your business and personal opportunities tenfold.

Perhaps you've already gone through the honeymoon stage of creating your business, but are struggling to establish yourself, typically due to a lack of clients. Perhaps you're teetering on the edge of a nightmare. Well, fear not. With the professional guidance in this book, you'll be able to save yourself and your dream. The authors of this book will take you on a journey to exploring how you can remain authentic, and build lifelong relationships. They'll show you how to avoid self-limiting beliefs, create a winning mindset, and navigate fear, to find your path. You'll learn how to fine tune your emotional intelligence, making real connections, and explore the latest time management tools to keep you on top of things. What more could you want?

Now it's up to you to take this opportunity and give it your all. You have everything you need here, in this book, to make it happen. You just have to take action and enjoy your adventure, as I am enjoying mine.

Speaker, Executive Coach and Mentor

www.leontaylor.co.uk

Leon is an Olympic Silver Medallist. After 20 years in elite sport, he has gone on to become the BBC's "Voice of Diving". In addition to coaching corporate clients and delivering workshops on a variety of high performance topics, he is also a valued mentor to Olympic and Paralympic athletes.

Speaker, Executive Coach and Mentor

www.leontaylor.co.uk

Introduction

By

David Mouro-Jones

Hello, my name is David Mouro-Jones. I'm the COO of IAPC&M, and a director of my own company. I'm so glad that you picked up a copy of this book, as I truly believe that the lessons contained within these pages are life-changing. Now, before we begin, let me provide you with a few business insights, from some experts in the field:

- *"Between 2007-2016, over 39,000 businesses failed within their first year."* – Rebecca Wilson, Recruitment International, 2017.
- *"Businesses fail for a whole number of reason, including: a lack of clear value proposition, no plan, no marketing platform, failing to act on marketing information, and poor management."* – Bernard Marr, Hiscox, 2016.
- *"Commonly sighted reasons why clients leave include: a lack of trust, no perceived value (ROI), failure to deliver what was promised, apathy and neglect, as well as budgetary reasons."* – Jason DeMerrs, Entrepreneur Europe, 2016.
- *"Customers want you to meet their expectations, solve their problems, give them contact options, and respond in a timely manner. They want to forge a relationship with you – and you should aim to do the same with them."* – Jason Bigue, Fonolo, 2014.

If the above list filled you with fear or trepidation, don't worry. Many an entrepreneur/ solopreneur has learnt these lessons the hard way, as have many SMEs and larger enterprises. The word "learn" is the key here. We can learn from failure, just as much as we can learn from success, which brings me onto my next point.

You might have noticed that the research I quoted doesn't include any information on how to win clients, or retain them. Well, this book addresses that dilemma. Without clients, you don't have a business – you have a hobby. So, this book provides you with the necessary knowledge, information, insights, and ability to successfully grow and develop your own business. It's an opportunity for you to learn from other people's mistakes, and what they did to correct them, as well as reading about the various strategies they adopted and adapted to enjoy success – many of which will help you develop your business too.

My thanks go to the authors for their commitment in producing a business handbook of the highest possible standard. They have dedicated time and shared their knowledge, because they are all passionate about helping solopreneurs to grow and sustain their businesses. The result is a book that many of them would have welcomed at the outset of their journey; I know I would have. In the process of reading this book, I have learned a great number of things, all of which I intend to apply to my own practice. You are never too experienced to learn from others, and I sincerely hope that you can take the messages contained within these pages and apply them to your own business.

CONTENTS

CHAPTER ONE

By

Adele McCormack

(A+V) x T = Clients

The Formula for Winning and Keeping Clients

When starting out as a solopreneur in the service industry, making money can seem like a huge mountain to climb. Completing training and gaining accreditation are only half the battle. You must then find people who are willing to pay for your services, and have longevity of clients to make your business sustainable. In this chapter I will introduce you to my formula for winning and keeping clients. It involves three essential characteristics:

To win clients, you need to be AUTHENTIC.

To be authentic, you need to have clear VALUES.

To keep your clients, they need to TRUST you.

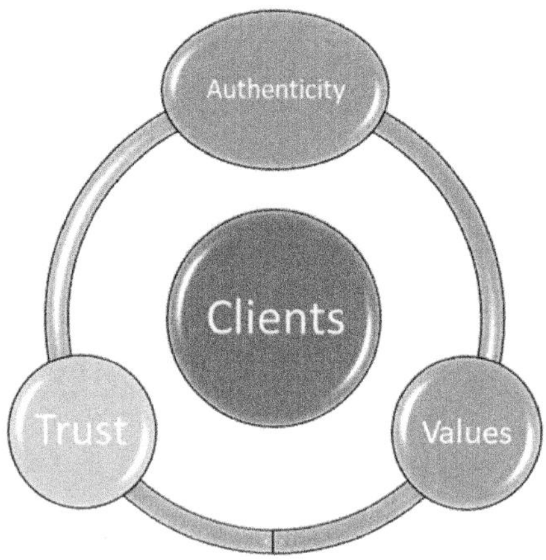

©*image* by *Adele McCormack*

These characteristics will fast-track your business to success, and guarantee to have you jumping out of bed each morning – pumped and rejuvenated. Without them, it will be a long, uphill battle.

While this may seem simple, in my experience it is easier said than done. Now, you may be wondering why anyone would struggle to be authentic, unless they were a fraud or trying to deceive. But many people do struggle. I struggled, and I struggled for a long time. Not because I wanted to trick anyone, but because, like many new business owners, I got lost in the big scary world of marketing. My marketing and branding bore no reflection on who I am as a person, what I believe, and how I operate. When I look back on some of my marketing spiel, it was dull, dull, dull. Did I attract any clients? Nope, not a single one! And if I saw my own advert, would I of bought from myself? No, nope, and never!

In this chapter, I am going to share with you the lessons I learned and the mistakes I made, so that you can fast-track yourself to success, and build a sustainable business. By the end of this chapter you will have a clear, consistent idea of how to market yourself online and in person, so that you are winning and keeping clients without even trying. In fact, you will love doing it. So, get yourself comfy, and let's begin.

Authenticity

"Authenticity is the alignment of head, mouth, heart and feet – thinking, saying, feeling and doing the same thing – consistently. This builds trust, and followers love leaders that they can trust." – Lance Secretan

A fundamental question that you must ask yourself, is: 'Would I invest in my own services, based on my advert?' If the answer is no, then please don't expect anyone else to buy from you. There are millions of other solopreneurs out there, all trying to make it big. How are you going to stand out from the rest, if you just sound like everyone else? If you are selling a service, then you are selling YOU. In order to sell yourself effectively, you need to build a connection and rapport with your target client group, from the moment they encounter you.

You are probably familiar with the business networking website LinkedIn. Think about when you are scrolling through, and someone catches your attention. What made that person stand out from the crowd? Was it their photo, something they said, or was it something else? You are more likely to connect with someone who is working in the same field, and who has similar interests, values, and ideas to you, than someone who is the total opposite.

Use this approach to think about marketing yourself in business. You want to attract the clients that you want to work with. You want to build a relationship with them, and you want the relationship to last. Relationships are built on trust, and you gain trust by being authentic. So, in order to win clients, you need to make sure the authentic YOU is shining through!

Pay Attention to Your Own Experiences

To help you get some clarity and actionable points, take notice about what stands out for you.

Action: Search the internet for something that interests you e.g. gym membership. Then, answer the following questions:

- **Q** What first draws you in? Is there a particular element which ensures that you stay on the webpage?
- **Q** What do you notice about the colours the advert uses? What do they mean to you?
- **Q** What language does the advert use? Which words stand out as important to you?
- **Q** What do you think the values of the company advertised are?
- **Q** How does the advert make you feel?
- **Q** Why would you buy their service/product?

Consider how you can apply this to your own marketing. If you are attracted to something, then this is a good indication that the marketing has worked, and therefore you can learn from this. For example, if you are drawn to a gym website because they use lots of visual images, and you are a visual person, then using visuals would be a good way to present yourself in your marketing. Don't stop paying attention to your own experiences. Keep a journal of them. You will gain some invaluable insights along the way.

When you have done this, and created your first wave of marketing/first website draft, or even if you are considering a rebrand, the next stage would be to ask other people for feedback. Don't be afraid to ask for help; just because you are a solopreneur does not mean you have to be on your own. Offer a discount or a free session for their time, if it makes you feel better.

Action: Get 10 people to look through your marketing. Choose 5 people who know you well, and 5 who don't. Ask them some questions:

- **Q** What does my marketing say to you?
- **Q** Based on my marketing, what would you say are my values?
- **Q** What does my marketing say about me?
- **Q** What are you most and least attracted to in my marketing?

When I first started marketing myself, I tried to be all stiff and professional; I thought that this would make people trust me and book me. But I didn't get a booking; not a sausage! This long, painful lesson, where the tumbleweed rolled along in the whistling wind, whilst the phone never rang, went on for about 12 months. So, let me save you that wasted time – let's get you to greatness quicker.

In my case, I realised that I needed to properly market my business, instead of just having a website, a phone that never rang, and an empty inbox. When I eventually found out about search engine optimisation, content marketing, and social media marketing, my head almost exploded! I stumbled across some online marketing webinars, and attended every one that I could. However, when I tried to put those methods into practice, it all felt a bit cliché – like I was following a script. I didn't believe in what I was writing, and that became evident in my content. Marketing became a chore, and I felt lost in the whole thing. I ended up with the typical case study advert, which lists endless questions like: "Have you ever felt like your life is in turmoil?", "Do you need help in finding your direction?" The content bored me to tears. Evidently, it bored potential clients too, and the phone remained silent. Let me give you an example of one of my earliest website revisions:

"Are you looking to make a big life change but need the courage to do so? Have you always wanted to start your own business but never seem to get over the first hurdle? Are you currently having to deal with a big life change and not sure which way to turn? When we are faced with adversity or challenges, it is important to understand the relationship you have with yourself. We can help you remove the blocks that are preventing you from achieving your fullest potential. Our coaching packages will be able to help."

The biggest problem with this text is that I am always referring to "our" and "us". I thought that if I presented myself as a big company, I would attract big business clients. So many people make this mistake. They try and hide behind an imaginary "team", but what they are really doing is hiding in the market. If you want to stand out in the crowd, then YOU need to step forward!

An important lesson is to stop pretending your business is something it is not. If there is only YOU in your business, then be the best YOU that you can be. Focus your energy on marketing who YOU are and what YOU offer, not what you think you ought to be:

- ✓ Be yourself.
- ✓ Be true.
- ✓ Be proud of being you.

I would describe myself as a high energy and positive person. I love to laugh and have fun. The content on the early version of my website was not a reflection of this, or me. Any potential customers would've had no idea who they'd be working with; no rapport had been built and no trust had been developed.

Imagine if you were looking for a therapist. Let's say, in this example, you wanted someone to help you deal with social anxiety. You would want to know who the therapist was, before you hired them. You would want to know what they offered, and how they could help you. But (and this is the bit people forget), you would also want to know why this person was the right fit for you. This last point is often done on gut feeling, which is generated through building rapport. Rapport is built through being authentic and having clear values. When you are authentic and have clear values, then this can help to create trust. Ultimately, it is authenticity, values, and trust, that wins clients.

My own lightbulb moment for generating authentic content came when I ran a retreat, in April 2017. I had always wanted to do this, and I met someone who wanted to facilitate with me. As we were both working with the same type of client group (people going through divorce), we settled on a divorce retreat. We found the perfect venue, set a date, parted with lots of money, and then went about marketing it. Unfortunately, we only had about 2 enquiries; even after relentlessly advertising on Facebook, Twitter, and through divorce lawyers, no one booked on. We even started to dread the idea of running it.

When we sat down and took a good look at the marketing, we both realised that there was nothing about this retreat that sounded remotely attractive. Neither of us would have wanted to attend, so why on earth should we have expected anyone else to? I go back to the earlier question; 'Would you invest in your own services based on your advert?' You need to keep this in mind at all times, when marketing.

At the same time, I stumbled across a content marketing duo called Andrew and Pete, based in the north of England. I say stumbled, but really they jumped out of Twitter and slapped me in the face. For any of you who use Twitter, you'll know that to really stand out you must do something remarkable, and in my opinion that is what Andrew and Pete did. They hooked me in with an automated direct message. I normally hate automated direct messages, however Andrew and Pete sent me a DM with a difference, and that is what made them stand out. Andrew and Pete's DM was different, because it was funny and quirky. Because of that, I visited their website, where they offered a free 30-minute session to work on my content. What they gave to me in 30 minutes was invaluable, and made me realise that I needed to stop trying to be boring and stiff, and start being me in business. In those 30 minutes I felt valued, understood, and as a bonus we laughed a lot! They never tried to "sell" to me in the traditional sense of the word, but they sold to me through the quality of their service. They were so good that they didn't need a sales script; they had already won me over just because they **didn't** sell. They were genuine and authentic. I trusted them, and I recommended them to loads of people **before** I had even purchased anything from them. How wonderful would it be for people to talk about the service **you** offer like that? Word of mouth can really help grow your business. If I talk about Andrew and Pete like this, then how many other people are doing the same? Andrew and Pete are my marketing heroes!

Action:

- **Q** What kind of hero do you want to be for your clients?
- **Q** When you've had a good service in the past, what was it that stood out about that service?
- **Q** What did you value about that service?

Now, think about how you can apply these qualities to your own business.

Andrew and Pete bowled me over with laughter, and now laughter is something I feature in my business. I went on to spend money with Andrew and Pete, and they delivered a great service. They gave me a lot to think about, and helped me realise what my brand values are. They helped me to realise where I am different to other solopreneurs, and how I could use this difference to stand out from other people.

Action:

- **Q** What are you doing that is different to other people offering the same service?
- **Q** How are you different to those people?
- **Q** What is unique about you?

Use these quirks and traits to help you stand out from the crowd!

I applied what I'd learned to marketing the retreat, and with only a month to go, we changed the entire focus. This seemed like a scary prospect, but I knew categorically that it was the right thing to do. My partner and I created a retreat that ***we*** would have liked to attend. We thought about what would make us book on a retreat, and we implemented a marketing strategy that would suit us, if we were potential clients. We called it the "Beautiful Souls Wellness Retreat". We talked about having a space to relax, quietening the mind and healing the heart, and promised lots of laughter and great food. The retreat sold out within 3 weeks, and everyone who came laughed a lot, forming lifetime friendships in the process. Because the marketing was authentic to who we are, we attracted attendees that we really liked working with, who we are still in touch with, and to whom we have continued to offer services and support if they need it. We went from having no bookings to having 11 people attend the retreat – a high-ticket item and a great return on investment. 5 months later, we ran a 1-day retreat. We used the same, if not similar wording, and another 14 people booked on, with 2 repeat bookers from the weekend retreat.

To really understand the difference in the marketing, let me share with you some of the initial text from our "Divorce Retreat", before we implemented our new strategies:

"When faced with the prospect of Divorce, you will experience a myriad of emotions. This can include anger, anxiety, and depression, feelings of low self-worth, relief, guilt and sadness. This Divorce Retreat offers a safe space for you to explore and work through the complexities of those emotions, to allow you to maintain your best self during the Divorce process."

The new text from the rejuvenated advert went something like this:

"The Beautiful Souls Wellness Retreat aims to heal hearts and minds, and offers you a space to breathe from the stresses of life, to emerge stronger and more confident by creating a lifestyle change of self-love and positivity, for personal growth and development. There will also be lots of time for fun and laughter, with creative opportunities to help you express yourself in your truest form. The retreats are small, so that you can relax, unwind, laugh, and connect with others."

As you can see, there is a complete change in language between the two advertisements. One is negatively focused, and the other is more positive. If you were going to part with some hard-earned cash, you would want to go to a retreat where you could relax, have fun, and be nurtured – not one where we were talking about how negative you feel when going through a divorce.

I also spoke to a good friend of mine, who was going through a messy divorce at the time, and her words spoke volumes to me. She said, 'To be honest, Adele, I don't want to think about my divorce, and I certainly wouldn't want to go on a retreat to talk about it. What I want is to heal my heart and stop my brain from working overtime. I want some time where I am not thinking about it.'

As you can see, much of what she said became part of our marketing. Whilst the new retreat was not specifically directed at people going through divorce, some of the attendees were dealing with the end of a marriage or long-term relationship. The important lesson here is to think about what your potential clients want. Also think about what you would want. Once again, I revert to the question at the beginning: would you invest in your own services based on your advert?

Action: Put together a focus group or speak to people individually who could be potential clients. Ask them what they would want/need from you. Ask them what would stand out in your marketing. Why not throw in a free session for their time? Deliver them a great service, and BOOM you've got a group of potential new clients!

Language is very important when it comes to your marketing, as it can invoke positive and negative feelings. However, when people are reading language, the tone or context of the narrative can sometimes be confused. When we wrote the initial "Divorce Retreat" advert, our intentions were to be empathetic and create the idea of a safe space for emotional exploration. As a coach, my job is to nurture not lecture, to empower not impose. These are my beliefs, and yet if you interpret the initial "Divorce Retreat" advert in the latter context, this is a complete contradiction of those beliefs. Even reading it back now makes me feel uptight. The "Beautiful Souls Retreat" advert reads so differently, and the clarity of my values is prominent.

When writing this chapter, I went back to some of our attendees and asked them what it was that made them book on our retreat, instead of another one. Here are some of the answers:

"When I looked at her website at the description of the retreat, I liked that there was no use of pretentious language and that it was completely approachable to somebody like me, who was new to the world of self-reflection." – Danielle

"I guess for me the attraction was the idea of having some time out to reflect on how life is going and what it could look like. I also thought you had chosen a beautiful venue, and I knew I would meet like-minded people, who inspire in different ways. This is so important for personal growth." – Emma

You will see from this feedback that both parties felt connected with the advert. It was clear and explicit, and it tapped into their values. The importance of not using "pretentious language", being "approachable" and meeting "like-minded people" were all strong features. This just shows how important it is to be authentic in your marketing.

It is not always about showing off your knowledge; it is about building rapport from the first moment. Our clients connected to our advert because our personalities were connected to that advert. The advert was an extension of us and our values – my partner and I were authentic, and this made it easy to promote.

Once I felt connected with the new retreat, I loved marketing it. I was thriving on it. I was passionate about it, and I was marketing every day, several times a day. I did Facebook live videos, blogs for Huffington post, online competitions; you name it I did it. When clients rang and asked about the retreat, I was pumped talking about it. I was telling anyone who would listen. I truly believed in what we were doing, and I was "selling" spaces without even realising that I was selling.

Passion is contagious. Take notice of how you are feeling when you are running your business. If you are waking up feeling passionate, inspired, and full of energy, this is fantastic. If you are putting barriers up, procrastinating, and feeling lethargic about your business, then something is conflicting with your values. You are not being authentic to who you are. You will need to address this and then make changes. It may seem easier to just keep pushing a boulder up a steep hill, rather than making a change, but if your business is draining you then you won't be at your best for your clients. Check out the values exercise (in the section about values) for help on this, as you will probably find that your values are not in line with your business.

If you are not getting clients in the beginning, don't internalise and sabotage. Often people feel that when they are not getting clients, it must be down to their skills. They lose confidence and throw in the towel, declaring themselves a failure. Let me tell you – failure is just a series of lessons to help make you great. If this is where you are at, please don't despair. The chances are, your business only needs a tweak.

How to Be Authentic

It may seem weird to teach you how to be authentic, but when you are starting out in a new business venture, there is a lot riding on it being a success. Perhaps you have stared for many hours at a blank page not knowing what to write, or rewriting something repeatedly to make it perfect. Being authentic is about more than just being at peace with your imperfections – it is about embracing them and trusting that you are perfectly imperfect. You are exactly as you are meant to be.

As trust is built on openness and honesty, if you are covering up those "imperfections" or character traits, then you are being the antithesis of open and honest. People will see through it, and it will be exhausting to maintain this "perfect" image that you are trying to portray. Once you have let go of this, you will feel freer, content will flow, and your business will be much easier to run. If, like me, you have an academic background, you may find it hard to shrug off an academic style of writing. And if you don't trust your own voice, then it might seem doubly hard. I am not saying that content should not be factual or backed up by evidence, but when you are selling a service you don't have 3000 words (plus references) to make an impact.

Action: You will need a timer, paper and pen, or computer (however you prefer to write).

Finding Your Authentic Voice
<u>Part A</u>: Set the timer for 10 minutes and turn off any distractions. At the top of the page, put the name of whatever it is your business is about: coaching, training, counselling, etc. Now write solidly for 10 minutes, noting everything you think about that topic. Do not stop to correct spelling or grammatical mistakes. Do not stop for anything, even if you write "I don't know what to write" repeatedly, just keep writing as quickly as you can until the time is up, ideas will come to the fore. Make sure that what you are writing is your opinion, not what you think you should write.
<u>Part B</u>: Repeat this process every day – 10 minutes per day, for a week. If you want to continue after the 10 minutes, don't stop. Keep writing until you feel you have come to a natural end.
<u>Part C</u>: Look back on what you have written over the last week. You should now see your voice emerge and have the makings of a good blog or good marketing content. Tweak and change as you desire, resolving any spelling or grammatical errors.
<u>Notes</u>: The more you get used to writing your opinion and views, the easier it becomes for you to stand out from the crowd, because your writing is more reflective of your personality. Repeat this process as often as you can, until you are able to write without that niggling voice in your head. This is also a really great way to blog. Blogs are normally approximately 500 words, which you will be able to generate very quickly using this method.

Trust yourself to be great – because you are.

Trust that you have a place in the market – because you do.

Stop comparing yourself to other people in your field – because they are not you.

Don't try and emulate other people – because you are not them.

Key Learnings:

- ✓ Let go of who you think you should be, and start being who you are.
- ✓ Take notice of how you feel. If you are not feeling passionate, then assess if you are going in the right direction.
- ✓ Failure is just a lesson, designed to make you greater. Embrace failure, and treat it as a learning curve.

Values

"Your beliefs become your thoughts, your thoughts become your words, your words become your actions, your actions become your habits, your habits become your values, your values become your destiny." – Gandhi

I have mentioned the importance of being true to your values when it comes to marketing. It is also imperative that your values are visible. Get into the habit of marketing what your values are, so that you can attract the clients that you want to work with. My 3 brand values are: **Energetic**, **Laughter** and **Smashing Glass Ceilings**. My talks and training sessions are always high energy. I love to inject laughter into anything (I am a laughter workshop facilitator – yes that really is a thing) and my passion is helping people to smash their glass ceilings. These values are representative of my personality and passions, and I lace them through all the content on my website, and in my marketing.

Writing about your values is a great way to generate content, and could be the foundation of many blogs that will help raise your profile. Pick values that make you stand out from the crowd. You can also use your values to create your own brand voice or lingo. For example, where someone else might talk about limiting beliefs, I talk about glass ceilings. This has become my branding lingo. You will see in Ruby's chapter that she talks about her "dreamie" clients. This is part of her branding lingo.

Image by mdadrf10 on Fiverr

Identifying Your Values Exercise

Part A

Think about a particular area of your business, and then answer the following question:

'What is important to me about the service I deliver?'

Continue to ask yourself the same question, until you have a thorough list. The important thing is not to overthink it; just keep writing until you feel you have your complete list.

Example:

'What is important to me about my service?'

What is important to me about my service?	➭	Trust
What else is important to me about my service?	➭	Quality
What else is important to me about my service?	➭	Value for Money
What else is important to me about my service?	➭	... and so on ...

Part B

Now, looking at your list, think about which aspect of that value is important to you. How would you describe it to someone else?

Example: Quality – this could mean ensuring the right skills to deliver the right service.

Or it could mean:

- Delivering a good service.
- Developing trust.
- Going above and beyond.

Go through your list and identify what each of those values mean to you.

Part C

Once you have a good list of values, have a go at putting them in order of importance.

Part D

Make a note of your top 3 values here:

Value Rank	Core Value	Description of the value

Notes: Consider the language that you would use to describe the things that are important to you, as opposed to how other people would describe them. Ambition is a huge value of mine, but describing this as "smashing glass ceilings" has a different impact. Smashing glass ceilings is about being more than just ambitious; it's about working with people who want to break the mould. When thinking about your values, consider how they can be described uniquely, because this will help you stand out.

Using Your Values in Marketing

Finding your values should be one of the first things you do when starting a business. That's not to say that you can't revisit and amend these values in the future, but when you look at blogs or websites that have clear values as opposed to just factual representations of the service they are delivering, they stand out more. You will see in Maria's chapter that she talks about winning hearts, to gain more clients. I totally agree with this concept, and being explicit about your values is a great way to do that.

When you have completed the "Identifying Your Values" exercise above, you can use your values to write your first 2 or 3 blogs relating to your business. When I started out, I was marketing myself as a Relationship Coach, and one of my brand values was laughter. So, I wrote a blog about how laughter can heal heartache. The purpose of this was to attract clients wanting to positively deal with the end of their relationship, as opposed to spending time on Facebook stalking their ex. If a client wanted to be passive in their recovery from heartbreak, my marketing would turn them away.

One of the most attractive things about becoming a solopreneur, is having a better working environment. It is therefore important to attract the clients that you want to work with, and that you will have fun working with. This also means turning away clients who you do not feel are best suited to you. Being explicit about your ideal clients right at the beginning ensures that you are attracting clients who you will have a better rapport with, and who are likely to rebook. Yes, it may mean that there will be people who don't book with you because of your marketing, but you cannot be everything to everyone. The more ambiguous you are in how you present yourself, the less interest in your services people will have. If you are too generic, then you will not build rapport with anyone. Being clear about your values will attract people who mirror those values. When you meet with them for the first time, you then can build that rapport further.

Your Elevator Pitch

In the very busy social media world, people have a short attention span. This means that you need to have a clear and concise elevator pitch that describes what type of people you help, and how you help them. You have 10 seconds to do it – AND you need to get your personality in there.

Example 1: 'I help people who feel stuck in a rut find clarity and purpose by offering 1:1 coaching sessions.'

Here, there is no clarity on who the service is aimed at, and how skilled you are at delivering the coaching.

Example 2: 'I work with professional women who feel held back in their careers, helping them to smash their glass ceilings and achieve world domination. After an intense 6-week course, my Rockettes can stage dive and crowd surf into the next level of their awesomeness.'

This gives greater clarity on who the service is for, and the personality of the person delivering the service shines through.

The brand values of "glass ceiling smasher", "energetic" and "laughter" are far more obvious in example 2. Some will love it, and some will hate it. But the ones who love it will be the ideal clients.

Nobody will love example 1!

Key Learnings:

- ✓ Finding unique ways to describe your values will help you stand out from the crowd.
- ✓ Use those unique descriptions to help create your branding lingo.
- ✓ Being explicit about your values helps attract clients who are better suited to you, and who you are likely to build the best rapport with.
- ✓ Create a 10-second elevator pitch describing your ideal client and incorporating your values.

Trust

"If people like you, they'll listen to you, but if they trust you, they'll do business with you." – Zig Ziglar

When buying a service or a product, you will only part with your money if you **trust** that you are going to **get** what you have paid for. Likewise, you will only part with money if you **trust** that what you have paid for is **good quality**, and if you **trust** the item or service to give you what you **want**.

When clients trust you, they will stay with you.

When you start to build rapport with a client, you start a relationship with them, and with that comes the need to build trust. Trust has so much significance and power when it comes to business, it can create beautiful relationships, and yet when broken it can destroy anything. By the dictionary definition, trust is described as, "The firm belief in the reliability, truth, or ability of someone or something."

A recent example of how a breach of trust can single-handedly destroy a business, is Cambridge Analytica. Broken trust ended existing business relationships and prevented new ones from forming, and the company went into administration – after being exposed by a whistle-blower. Prior to the scandal, business had skyrocketed; Cambridge Analytica were working with Facebook, the Trump presidential campaign, and the UK's Brexit campaign. After the scandal broke, the public trust in the business was in tatters, and this extended to any associations of the business. Facebook in particular was left clinging to a cliff edge, and this has had far-reaching repercussions for the whole industry.

When running a business, you need to consider the 3 dimensions of trust, in order to be successful:

1. Trusting yourself.
2. Trust for your business.
3. Trust in the industry.

Trusting Yourself

Trusting yourself is key to generating content that is authentically you, and is your key to success. When you don't trust yourself, you become fearful, and that fear will hold you back – time and time again. I bet that when you really think about what you are afraid of, there is nothing that tangible.

Let me give you an example from my coaching practice. I once worked with a lady who had a dream of setting up her own counselling practice. She had the qualifications, the accreditation, and many years of experience working as a counsellor. The reason why this had remained a dream, and had not become a reality for her, was because she did not trust that she could set up a business and get clients. The irony was that she was already managing a counselling service for an organisation. When she started the job, the service didn't exist, and so she set it up from scratch. She had already done it, and it was a great success. However, having a boss and someone to whom she was accountable were the things that drove her to succeed as an employee. In her mind, she didn't feel able to actually set up for herself.

Going out on your own can be scary, and can feel incredibly lonely. There is a lot of perceived uncertainty, and with that comes self-doubt. People lose sight of who they are, and try to "become" something they are not. I've shared with you that in the initial stages of my business, I tried to make everything so formal, in the belief that I would attract more business clients that way. However, providing a service does not mean that you have to be boring. Professionals, directors, and CEOs like to have fun too. They may want a high energy coach or trainer who will throw in a laughter workshop for the graveyard shift after lunch. After all, why not? When you start trusting yourself and being yourself, you will start to win big in business, and building your business will become easy.

My initial work was focused around divorce and relationship coaching, but I was struggling to keep writing about the subject. I started to pick up work from other known associates to do coaching with women about changing jobs, leaving jobs, setting up businesses, and progressing in their careers. I also got asked to do some work with young adults, focusing on careers and goalsetting. This got my blood pumping; this was the stuff that was making my heart sing, and my clients were getting better outcomes. I was becoming better at what I did, by doing the things that I loved. If you love what you are doing and are passionate about it, then you will build rapport and trust with your clients at a far quicker rate.

If you've ever been served by someone who loves their job, and trusts themselves to be good at their job, you will know about it. They will give you a better service, and you are more likely to revisit them. As a personal example, I was sorting out my car insurance one day, when I got someone on the end of the phone who was clearly not interested in his job. I rang another company and got a lady called Sian, who couldn't have been more helpful. We even laughed and joked whilst sorting it out (laughter always gets me – I am a cheap date!) At the end of the call, I had bought my car insurance from her company and I rang back 4 months later with my home insurance and partner's car insurance to create a multi-cover. Sian clearly loved her job; her passion came through on the call and she built rapport and trust with me as a customer. She turned what would have been a £300 policy into a £1000 policy – the difference it can make when you love what you do. If you do not love what you are doing, then no one else will. Trust your gut. Trust yourself and make the necessary changes so that you **do** love your job. It is not a failure if you have to change things up; it's a lesson on your path to greatness. Trust yourself, and believe that you are great.

Trust for Your Business

As in any relationship, trust is something that must be built over time. A good way to do this, when you are not able to meet potential clients face to face, is to write articles. This way you are demonstrating to the audience that you have knowledge about your topic, and offering the reader the chance to hear your "narrative" and conversation style. Imagine that you had 2 maths teachers, who both explained the same problem, but in differing ways. One teacher makes the problem seem difficult, whereas another teacher makes it quite simple. Which would you prefer? Reading your articles and blogs will draw clients to you, because you explain their problem in a way that they understand. And the more you write, the more trust you build up.

If you don't feel comfortable with writing, or you are time limited, then make videos, tweet, or post photos. Start with what you feel most comfortable doing, but do lots of it. Don't panic about whether it sounds right or looks right, because the more you try to tweak and change it, the more chance there is of your personality getting lost. Try a Facebook live video. Don't have a script, just have a general idea of what message you want to give, and go for it. It doesn't have to be lengthy – 20 seconds is enough – just as long as it puts the message out there. I suggest Facebook live, for the very reason that it is *live*. You are on with an audience, and the real you will shine through. It's ok to say 'um' and 'ah', because that is all part of normal conversation. The more you are YOU, the quicker you will build trust and rapport.

Some people opt for trying to create trust by writing "I am the leading expert on this subject". And whilst there are genuine leading experts out there who do this, some people just use this as a lazy way of marketing themselves. If the proof is not in the pudding, then you will not get booked again. Your business will then become unsustainable, because it is harder to keep booking new clients if you are unable to retain any. The title of being "a leading expert" is one that should be earned and given to you by your peers, not something you give to yourself. If someone markets themselves as the "leading expert" on a certain topic, I want to know what they have done or have achieved to be considered the leader in their field. A leading doctor for example, would have to demonstrate that they've had many years of training and experience, contributing to their field considerably with research, and performing their specialty for thousands and thousands of hours with huge amounts of success. Other doctors and people in the medical profession would look up to them, and they would be contributing to improving the profession by being involved in research, teaching, and writing of academic papers. If you are marketing yourself as the "leading expert" then you need to be doing all those things, and have the evidence to back it up.

A good way to create trust is by being focused on good customer care. The biggest brands put huge emphasis on this. Therefore, the same consideration needs to be given for small businesses. Just because you are a solopreneur, does not mean that you shouldn't have robust policies in place to deliver great customer care. A client needs to know that there is minimal risk to their investment, and that their consumer rights are protected.

When I am securing a new client, I am very open and frank with people about my complaints policy. It is important for the client to know that they are protected. This initial conversation has even helped secure several clients in the past; one example was someone who'd had a poor experience with a counsellor. I was able to show all my qualifications, and the procedure of my accrediting body that they could seek advice from if they were not happy with my service. Another example was securing work from someone who was a solicitor, and who expected these things to be in place – as they would be for his work. Had I not had all this in place, I could've lost that business.

Be explicit about your qualifications and accreditations. After all, you have worked hard to achieve these, so shout about them! All of this will help build credibility in your business, and demonstrate that you have been through a robust assessment of your skills. Prospective clients will know that they are protected, and will be more likely to book you over someone else.

Trust in the Industry

As a solopreneur, you are working with people and their lives. They are paying hard-earned money for you to help them, and they need to know that they can get the best outcome for themselves. You owe it not only to the client, but to your profession, to ensure this happens for every client. When there are examples of bad service, it impacts all the other people working in that field. If the public starts to lose trust in a service, then the industry takes a hit. Think of all the high-profile cases where public trust has been broken:

- Harold Shipman (GP serial killer in UK found guilty of murdering 15 patients) – public mistrust in GPs.
- The death of Baby P (died after suffering 50 injuries over an 8-month period) – public mistrust in social workers.
- Larry Nassar (American gymnastics team doctor found guilty of abusing hundreds of female athletes) – public mistrust amongst elite sporting teams.

Now, I am not writing about this to scare you – I am trying to show how one person's malpractice can singlehandedly create public mistrust in the profession, and could end up hindering your business. If the public consider your type of service to be the best thing for solving specific issues or problems, then your profession will flourish. You have a role to play in creating this public trust. Make sure you have robust policies in place, so that your clients feel safe and secure. Make sure you deliver exceptional customer care, so that you are the person they return to if they need the service again. Every time someone gets a good level of service from you, you are helping to maintain public trust and confidence within your service industry.

Consider linking up with other service professionals in your area. How can you work together for the benefit of all? Perhaps you get a prospective client, but you are not a good fit. Don't leave the client in the cold. Who do you know that you can refer them on to? Make the customer's whole experience and entrance into your industry a good one. Think about what else you can do to contribute to your profession. Contributing will raise your profile, make you better at what you do, and put you many steps forward to becoming a peer endorsed "leading expert". Then you will be able to secure new clients, and retain existing ones, without needing to try.

Key Learnings:

- ✓ There are 3 dimensions to trust: trusting yourself, trust for your business, and trust in the industry.
- ✓ Trust that what you are doing is right. If it feels wrong and you have lost the passion, then trust yourself to change what you are doing.
- ✓ Making a client feel protected, and ensuring they know there is minimal risk to their investment, will help build trust.
- ✓ You have a responsibility to contribute to your profession, to help build public trust and confidence.
- ✓ Contributing helps build your credibility.

Summary

Presuming you've read this chapter, then you certainly are passionate about making your business a success. Well done, and I wish you all the best in your future endeavours. My final thoughts and reminders to you are as follows:

- ✓ Know that you are good enough, you are capable, and there is a place for you in your industry.
- ✓ Trust in yourself that you are great, and that you are going to be successful. If things don't work, it is not a failure, just a lesson to make you great again. Don't throw in the towel, perhaps something just needs tweaking.
- ✓ Keep revisiting your values until you know with absolute certainty that they are your true values.
- ✓ Develop your own brand lingo/voice to help you stand out from the crowd, and give your business an identity.
- ✓ Keep the fire in your belly burning. If the fire starts to go out, you might need to re-build it in a different way.

Call to Action

Now you are ready to smash your glass ceilings and be super awesome at building your business. When you start smashing those glass ceilings, give me a shout out on Twitter, Facebook, Instagram, or LinkedIn. Alternatively, if you need a leg-up to smash that ceiling, then drop me a line at adele@northhousecoaching.com.

BUT don't leave here without at least one smashed ceiling!

Biography

Adele McCormack is an accredited coach with the IAPC&M, and their Head of Professional Standards. She is also a qualified Social Worker and trained laughter workshop facilitator. (Yes, there is such a thing!)

Adele began her coaching journey after a significant turning point in her life. Unhappy at work and at home, and living an unhealthy lifestyle, things looked bleak. However, a change in circumstance gave Adele the opportunity to train as a coach, and her life has since transformed. She's completed 2 marathons, 4 half marathons, 2 mud runs, had two children, flown a plane, got a job promotion, and is a "leading expert" in bouncing around the room like an idiot.

Adele has a fascination with helping #glassceilingsmashers and believes #anythingispossible. People do extraordinary things daily, and there is no reason why that cannot be YOU. If you need a smashing good time and have stratospheric ambitions, then please get in contact: www.northhousecoaching.com.

CHAPTER TWO

By

Lorna Phillips

Your Spiritual Guide to Finding Your Ideal Clients
***Without* Searching For Them!**

"The key to becoming a master of the material world is to become aware of how the energy of creation simultaneously flows through us and is us." – Ernest Chu

Michael Strong, CEO and Chief Visionary Officer of FLOW[i] once wrote, "[i]n the language of business, each human being who is dispirited is a loss to the balance sheet of global goodness, whereas each human being who is an inspired, energetic, and thoughtful change agent is an enormous asset to global goodness."[ii]

Think about that statement for a moment. Are you an inspired, energetic, and thoughtful change agent? Are you an asset to global goodness? No doubt you want to be, that's why you invested precious time, resources, and energy in training to be a coach, consultant, or other professional. It's also the reason why you are reading this book. At this moment though, you may be feeling dispirited, as you wonder how to get started in your new business, how to get your practice out of a rut, or how to build and retain your clientele.

If you are looking to change your mood from dispirited, confused, and overwhelmed, to optimistic, confident, and calm, and with it produce clients, wealth, happiness, and wellbeing, this chapter offers you a spiritual road map.

Your Road Map to Success

In this chapter you will be introduced to your steady and unchanging source of order, composure, and power – the Universe – and you will learn how to access this unlimited source via your higher-self (your perfect business partner). Imbued with re-discovered wisdom, you will be gently piloted to your three spiritual catalysts (your business partners) that when used in harmony will spur the manifestation of new clients, speaking engagements, writing opportunities, business opportunities, and more. With practise, you will develop clarity, confidence, and prowess, and over time will demonstrate mastery in the achievement of lasting success.

Your Tools

You will need to be a willing participant for this process; learning the spiritual principles of success is not a spectator sport. You will need the following:

- A journal. (You can use anything from a basic exercise book to an expensive designer leather-bound book. It's up to you, but what works for me is using something beautiful or elegant – something that reflects my vision for myself as I create my success.)
- A pen.
- The willingness to suspend judgment.

- A lack of ego. Seriously, send it into the next room to hang out for a while.
- A large mug of herbal tea, or other non-caffeinated or non-alcoholic beverage that you enjoy – you don't want to be jittery during this process.

Now, pin a *do not disturb* sign on your door, put your device on silent, settle down in your favourite armchair, and let's begin.

Your Perfect Business Partner – Your True Self

The first thing to figure out is who you are. Are you your body, your fashionable, quirky, or outdated wardrobe, your car, your profession, your race, or ethnicity? What about the house you live in, the qualifications you've earned, or the titles you've received? What about your name, your beautiful singing voice, or your gift for making people laugh? Are these you? What about your mind, or even your brain – through which you process your thoughts, construct, and interpret symbols as language, and pump the blood around your body? Your brain determines your actions. So, is your brain you? Are your thoughts you?

> **Journal**
>
> What external symbols of power have you invested your emotions in?
>
> How have they served you?
>
> Do you feel empowered or diminished?
>
> Which ones make you feel empowered and which diminished?
>
> What part has your ego played in your investment?

The answer, of course, is no. None of the characteristics described above are "you". They are manifestations or expressions of your existence. Some are circumstantial; they exist outside of your physical existence, and contribute to the circumstances of the life you live, such as your house and your car. Others are societal constructs bestowed upon you with your tacit agreement or participation, and to which you may or may not ascribe meaning; they include titles and qualifications. Some are incidents of birth, such as your nationality or race. Others, however, are existential and more closely related to the expression of your personality, or a physical skill such as your artistic talent or athletic ability. However, a quality they all share is that they are symbols of an externally defined power. Their authority or power is derived externally (i.e., by others), and they are temporary. They are either destructible or can be lost, stolen, sold, or withdrawn.

To become attached to, or inappropriately invest psychologically or emotionally in any of these characteristics, is to confine oneself to a life of uncertainty, insecurity, and inevitable failure. Any one or more of these characteristics, by their very nature, will fail you at some point. And if you have mistakenly defined yourself as any of them, it follows that when **it** fails, you will believe that **you** have failed. Think of businesspeople or investors that you may know or have read about, who feel that their identity is lost when their business fails or the stock market crashes. Why is this the case? The answer is, because they've made the mistake of letting something other than their true self define who they are.

Journaling

At various points in this chapter, I will invite you to reflect in your journal, by sincerely asking yourself the questions posed, and writing down the answers as they come to you. Take all the time you need, and be ruthlessly but compassionately truthful. Listen to your body. Take note of any tightness, shortness of breath, or other changes. If you're not sure of the answer to any question, leave it and come back to it another time. Your mind will keep working on the response and present it to you when it is good and ready.

'But if I am not these external symbols, and I am not my personality, then who am I?'

The above question is probably one of the most important ones you will ever ask, and you are not alone in asking it. It has occupied the wisdom traditions for many centuries. And, while the teaching is accessible, it seems it has to be deliberately sought out by most of us. However, the truth is hiding in plain sight; it is available for you to know right now.

Have you ever wondered how you know anything that you know? How do you know that you are reading these words right now? Who is it that knows? If you were to ask yourself right now, 'Who is reading this book?' then no matter what your response to that question would be, there is a part of you that quietly observes, that doesn't get involved in whether your answer is true or false, right or wrong. But it watches, and it knows. You can try this out with any activity you are engaged in. Just by paying close attention to yourself, you will realise that as you are doing whatever you are doing, there is "someone" watching you, that is not the part of you that is doing the activity.

That watcher is referred to by spiritual teacher and author Deepak Chopra as "the witness". You will have also heard it referred to as "the higher self". Your witness is completely reliable; it is non-judgmental, quiet, and ever-present. Your higher self is the permanent, unchanging, durable part of you that goes beyond personality or ego, or anything that your personality or ego might wish to associate with or attach to – be it money, people, things, or even aspirations or dreams, no matter how lofty and well-meaning. Your higher-self, my friend, is your spiritual identity. When you have found your spiritual identity, you've found your perfect business partner and your pathway to success.

The reason it's possible to identify this as your pathway to success, is because your spiritual identity is your connection to the Cosmos, the Universal Spirit, the Universal Mind. This "Universal Spirit" as I will call it, is the ultimate source of your being, your intelligence, your wisdom, your knowing, and yes, your success. You may have heard it described as the "field of all possibilities", which expresses the limitlessness of the creative process. Well, it is from this field that all of creation emanates, and from which all creations of brilliance (including the not so brilliant!) are born. And there are certain qualities inherent in the Universal Spirit which are inherent in you. They are: Wholeness, Life, Love, Light, Power, Peace, Beauty, and Joy.

One of the significant elements of the Universal Spirit, particularly relevant for the purposes of business development, is growth. There is a life-affirming energy that is continually pressing for expansion and expression. When you have the urge to create something, be it a painting or a new business service or product, or a new way to attract fresh clients, it is this creative energy that is seeking to express itself through you! Every single business idea, every invention, every creative endeavour (including this book), came into being because of the universal creative force. You see, your ideas have a genesis, and just like every business, they began as a brilliant idea. If you follow the steps set out in this chapter correctly, your ideas will manifest in fine style.

Overcoming attachment

'You're right. I do have some great ideas, really brilliant ones sometimes, but then I begin to doubt myself and get lost in negativity.'

As human beings, we are imbued with the gift of choice (unlike lower animals that are driven largely by instinct). Our lives are like a giant maze, and at each turn we must decide which pathway to take, leaning upon the clues that we either find along the way, or that seem to appear from nowhere. Learning how to navigate the maze of life requires us to learn and apply the Universal Laws that are discernible to all of us. We do this by connecting to our higher self. When we make choices, we do so either in compliance with the Universal Laws or not, and the results we get, determined as they are by our choice, will signal to us the accuracy or otherwise of our compliance. Often though, we fail to appreciate the Law.

Take our apparent inclination to become attached to things, people, or memories. For instance, if a bad thing happened to us in the past, we tend to identify with it, defining it as "us". Then we spend our time and energy trying to prevent it from ever happening again. In the process, we tell and re-tell the horror story to whoever will listen (including ourselves!) as if obsessed. It's an obsession that eventually possesses us. I'm sure you can think of at least one such story, we all have them. Perhaps you were once fired from a job, or an early business venture failed dramatically. At a moment's notice, you may be able to bring the experience vividly to mind, just as if it were occurring now. The truth is, the story or sequence of events may well have been awful at the time. It may have been frightening to you, and shook you up. But if you remember your spiritual identity, and that **you** are not the experience, then you'll find that your witness or spiritual identity is not shaken or afraid. You only become frightened when you engross yourself in your memory, and use your imagination to re-create your memories – putting them into a future that hasn't yet arrived. In other words, you frighten yourself with an illusion!

One strategy a coach might use to help such a client, is to invite him or her to re-contextualize the perceived problem. This has a way of loosening the mind's grip on the situation as he or she has defined it. In the above image, the man depicted experienced business venture failure. But, as we know, this does not make the man a "failure". So, when a client of mine found himself in a similar situation, I asked him what he learned from the experience, and what he would do differently today. I helped him understand the so-called problem by looking at it from a different perspective. Soon, he was able to see the event with neutrality, and as a positive, even necessary, experience. He was able to use it to help him perform even better than before, having now learned what did not work. His "I'm a failure" story was replaced with a self-awarded badge of honour, especially when I reminded him about some of entrepreneur mogul Richard Branson's spectacular business failures. And he grinned widely when I told him of Branson's alleged business motto, 'Screw It. Let's do it!' Suddenly, new possibilities began to spring up in my client's mind.

Overcoming Fear

You can try Activity A (which I will explain in-depth shortly) when you feel fearful of taking what you know is an important step in your business development, such as making that important follow up call to a prospective client, but you are haunted by a perceived past failure or embarrassment. Perhaps your first assignment or presentation didn't go over as well as you would have liked, and you cringe every time you think about it, or your proposal for a potentially lucrative assignment was not accepted. In any case, you could torment yourself with stories about your inadequacy and tell yourself that you likely won't win this client either, or you could change the past story to one that makes you feel better. It doesn't matter whether you change it to one that is true or not. Since neither story, your original one nor the replacement one is objectively true, go ahead and make it up! Make it elaborate, make it funny, laugh heartily at yourself, and then move on and make the call. With practise, you won't need a story; events will occur, and you won't define them as good or bad or even take them seriously anymore. Remembering the Universal Law of non-attachment to things, people, events, or memories, you will simply move on to the next adventure. Sometimes a story can be embedded so deeply in the subconscious that the person isn't even consciously aware of it anymore.

True story: At a recent workshop, a participant shared with me that she needed to make money for a project she wanted to get off the ground. However, she also expressed some ambivalence about money in general, claiming that while a lot of money had come her way during her early adulthood, for some reason she could never hold onto it. I noticed that her facial expression changed whenever she said the word 'money'. Upon deeper probing, it emerged that in her younger years many of the people she socialised with were from well-to-do families, some of whom appeared to demonstrate values she didn't share or care for. In her young mind, she associated those values with wealth and associated money (which of course being a symbol of external power has no intrinsic value) with negativity. No wonder she had disdain for money! With this deeply buried story brought to her conscious awareness, she now has an opportunity to dissolve the association and get on with the business of making her project a reality.

Journal

What stories are you telling yourself about your ability to attract clients, your knowledge, your intellect, skills, or your other attributes?

Are those stories consistent with you achieving success?

What stories are you committing to never re-telling again, either to yourself or anyone else?

To shed the sometimes debilitating habit of storytelling, one must live more consistently in the present moment. This requires a stilling of the mind. In this state of presence, one becomes conscious of being – aware of one's essence and one's connection to the source of creation. At the point of connection to your higher self, your story will disappear. Take every opportunity to remind yourself that the story is just that – a story you are telling yourself. Then stop doing it!

Suggestion: Probably one of the best methods for learning the art of presence is meditation. If you have never learned this, make a point of learning it very soon. If you know how to meditate, but it is not a common practice, then make it a regular activity. When done regularly, you will be able to attain presence on call, which in turn will positively influence every aspect of your life, including your business.

The key is non-attachment, and not assigning labels to an experience, whether good or bad. Remind yourself regularly that your source is spirit and that the Universal Laws that apply to the Universe (love, life, power, peace, joy, creativity, etc.) also belong to you, and they are available to you whenever you decide to remember your spiritual identity, whenever you return to being conscious, whenever you bring yourself to the present moment. It takes practise. Every time your mind strays into negative terrain, remind yourself to bring it back to the present moment. It's like pressing the reset button of your mind. And when you do, your wisdom, brilliance, creativity, and genius can stream to you, unhindered. Try it. Try it now. You will likely be stunned by the business ideas that come to you, filling you with excitement to get started.

Activity A: Try this (having someone read it to you might be more effective). Think of a problem that is bothering you. You have it? Ok, good. Now I want you to pick up an item in front of you. This could be anything, a book, a pen, or something else. Hold the article in your hands and look at it very carefully. Pay very close attention to it, just as if you are seeing it for the first time. Look at the colour, notice the shade, and notice where the colour changes varies in shade and brightness. Feel its texture, notice any markings or writing, and notice the patterns. Does the item have a smell? What is the sound it makes when you run your fingers over it or play with it? Look at it without judgment or comment. Just notice it deeply. Do this for a few moments. Now, put the item down.

When you were looking at the item, where was your problem? You may notice that it appeared to have left you, temporarily. Has it gone? Or did it not exist? The truth lies somewhere in the middle: it exists in its present form only as a machination of your mind. It is created in your mind and given emotional intensity by the attachment of meaning that you give to it. However, when you learn to bring yourself to the present moment, you immediately know that the spiritual you remains completely unharmed or untouched.

Discerning Your Spiritual Purpose

'I understand now how to access my higher self – my business partner – and through this medium I will get great ideas. But how will I know which idea to implement? Which one is best for me?"

Answer: Something will resonate deep in your soul. Certain ideas will have a meaning to you that others won't, and when you notice that a certain idea just keeps coming up for you, you will experience a sense of desire to get on with it that simply won't leave you alone.

True story: I was about 24 years old when my spiritual purpose became clear to me. From that day to this, it has been the driving force behind most of my conscious choices

– certainly those related to my professional and affiliated activities anyway. Note that I used the term, "conscious choices". I would be misleading you if I were to give the impression that all my behaviour since then has been conscious – it certainly hasn't!

The day my spiritual purpose became clear, I was reading a tattered old book given to me by a friend. It was called *I Write What I Like* and contained a collection of writings by Steve Biko. Mr. Biko was an anti-apartheid activist, who was brutally murdered by South African state security officers when they detained him for his involvement with the South African Students' Organisation, an anti-apartheid organisation. While I cannot recall the precise words he used in his book, he said something along the lines of: "The police can batter my body with their batons and boots, they can even kill my body, but my spirit will forever remain intact, unharmed and I live on victoriously." Maybe he had already glimpsed his earthly fate.

I remember this take on the immortality of spirit hitting me like a bolt of lightning – those words immediately resonated. My purpose was revealed to me as "becoming conscious and assisting others to do the same." Months later, I was offered work that enabled me to develop the skills that I use today, in the expression of that purpose.

Experiencing lasting success comes with ascertaining and remaining in alignment with your purpose. If you cannot name your spiritual purpose, here is my suggestion for where you should search. It is apparent that it lies somewhere in the giving of yourself, not for personal reward or recognition, but a greater good – a good beyond yourself or those connected to you, such as your family, friends, or tribe. It lies in selfless service and the sharing of your inner gifts for the good of others, the environment, or the world. When you are in selfless service, you will feel connected to your higher self, your business partner, and ultimately to the Universe. This philosophy is expressed by Kartar Singh Khalsa, CEO of Yogi Tea, who believes that businesses that are self-serving and even damaging to society have a limited life span in most cases. In contrast, he claims that organisations that survive are those that truly deliver service to society, enhancing the quality of our lives and enhancing our sense of what is possible. Khalsa's view is that "[t]he purpose of life is to serve. Through service, you can move from individual consciousness, through group consciousness, to universal consciousness."[iii]

That being said, don't worry if you can't yet name your spiritual purpose. It is enough for now to know that you are spiritual in nature. Also, know that through the practise of presence, and giving beyond yourself, you are living your spiritual nature every day, with the added bonus that you will feel good doing it. Activities, opportunities, and projects will show up that have meaning to you, and your unique character will develop the characteristics to match in equal measure the tasks required of you.

Journal

Do you have a personal mission? What is it – can you say?

Is the work you are seeking to be successful in now, in alignment with your personal mission?

Do you feel a passion for the work you do or the business you are considering?

Do you feel energised by your vision?

Is your vision somehow connected to the greater good, to the good of humanity or the planet?

Knowing your spiritual purpose really helps to push you through the fear. Knowing that what you are doing is the authentic expression of you, and your reason for being here, is often just the juice you need to get you going when negative energy threatens to stymie your plans. Even when you feel the fear, you can do it anyway!

Key Learnings:

Let's review some of the themes we've covered so far:

- ✓ Consciousness connects you to the very essence of who you are (your higher self) and to the source of all creation.
- ✓ Your higher self is your perfect business partner.
- ✓ Being in a state of consciousness or awareness enables you to overcome fear.
- ✓ You are not your house, your car, your name, your qualifications, or your title: your higher self is your spiritual identity.
- ✓ Re-contextualize a perceived problem, as a way of loosening its grip on your mind. Options include, changing the story or stopping telling it all together.
- ✓ The key to being conscious is practise, bringing yourself to the present moment as often as you can, but especially when things seem uncertain.
- ✓ Get in touch with and remain in alignment with your spiritual purpose, by searching for what brings meaning.

Your Three Powerful Business Allies

Now that you have located your spiritual business partner, and know how to align with your co-creator (the Universe), you are well positioned with brilliant business ideas – all of which are matched to your purpose. You are now raring to go. However, you are not there yet. There are three powerful business allies that you should seek out:

#1: Intention

The role of intention is to connect your business ideas or plans, with the aim of having them manifest into something tangible, and to help you be of service to your intended clients, even though you might not yet know who they are. The characteristics of intention, include: creativity, decision-making, clarity, quiet determination, consistency, steadfastness, courage, detachment, flexibility, integrity, and trust.

Intention is a process rather than an end, and involves you invoking it in an interaction with the creative and intentional energies inherent in the Universe. As explained earlier, the Universe already carries the invisible seeds of creation, and with them the essential ingredient of intention. Those seeds merely await the activation of **your** mind to engage with it appropriately, for results to manifest. This is how everything is created. Buildings. Inventions. Businesses. Ideas. Thoughts. Coaching and consulting practices. It is also how we create.

Intention is greater than desire, no matter how strong your desire is, since all your desire may amount to is wishful thinking or daydreaming, which lacks the psychic input required to invoke the power of creation. On the other hand, activating intention requires no force of will, no strenuous application, and no manipulation. Connecting your intention to that of the Universal Cosmic Intention assures you the success you seek, with minimal effort.

Bringing Clients to You with Your Intention

'So what exactly is this cosmic force you speak of, called intention?'

Spiritual teacher Carlos Castaneda explains intention as a force that exists in the Universe, while Dr. Wayne Dyer says it's a field of energy that flows invisibly beyond the reach of our normal everyday habitual patterns. However one describes it, it bears repetition that the Universe is a creative, interactive, intelligent, infinite cosmic energy, and we are microcosms of it, with minds that create. In other words, the Universe already has the power of intention built into it; whatever we intend or decide upon, the Universe as our co-creating partner has already conspired with us to bring it into being.

This is a stunning revelation. When you truly grasp the enormity of it, and its potential for conscious application in your life, you will understand how to bring your clients, your wealth, and your heart's desires into being, just by your intentions. Think about some of the rags to riches entrepreneurial legends. People such as Oprah Winfrey, Christopher Darden (whose life story was dramatised by actor Will Smith (also a legend) in the film "The Pursuit of Happiness", Starbuck's Howard Schultz, fashion designer Ralph

Lauren, and of course many others. Was it magic? Did they apply Herculean effort? No, it was neither – instead it was the appropriate application of intention, whether they were aware of it or not. Try it for yourself. Practise Activity B. Set up a vision board or something similar, to remind you of the outcomes you are envisioning for yourself.

Permit me to make one thing clear at this point: each of these legends will tell you that they had to work very hard, and they probably did. But don't get confused, what they will have worked hard at is mastering their craft and learning the business. Know that there is no substitute for becoming a master, in whatever product or service you provide. You must be on your A game. Clients will quickly realise if you do not know your craft, and you cannot fake it. You must work relentlessly at building your skills, just as the legends did. Similarly, you must maintain your professionalism and integrity, which means keeping alignment between your thoughts, your words, and your deeds. It also means striving to do no harm to others. When you fail to act honestly, or with integrity, it creates an energetic deficit in the Universe, which must be repaid by you at some point, in some way.

> **Journal**
>
> How do you ask for your success?
>
> Do you do so from a place of need or want?
>
> Consider re-energising your prayer from a place of gratitude, as if success is already yours.
>
> How does it feel different?

How to "Ask" the Universe for What You Want

'But why is it that when I ask for things, I don't seem to get them?'

The answer to this question is simpler than you think. There is an energetic difference between asking for something and intending it. Usually, the psychic energy associated with asking or pleading comes from a place of lack – a lack of confidence or a lack of self-worth. The Universe doesn't speak English or French or Swahili or Urdu, it communicates with the universal language of energy. So, when your words or even your thoughts are infused with the energy of lack, the Universe will give you results produced at the same level of energy. Thus, if you come from a place of wanting, what will be reflected to you is more wanting. You can think here of the beggars on the streets of Calcutta, Manhattan, or London. Their lives are not likely to change, even if they engage in a lifetime of begging. And I am sure you've heard stories of people winning the lottery, who within a relatively short period have lost their sudden wealth and are right back to the income level they were experiencing before their wealthy interlude. It's because the energy level at which their communications are vibrating hasn't changed. The energy that will attract the good things they seek, such as money, clients, love, or happiness, vibrates at a higher level.

If you are not getting what you want, the trick is to set your intention, and at the same time raise your energy to one that is confident, self-assured, and strong. If you do this, the Universe will respond accordingly. It's no accident that confident people are generally more successful. Now you know why.

By now, you may have realised that you have the power to create the reality you desire. You create your intentions, and step into alignment with your purpose or vision. The Universe will not judge you as good or bad, deserving, or undeserving. This is why you will see people whose values you do not share enjoying the fruits of their creation, and you may wonder how they have come to deserve such pleasures. It is your judgment that determines that they are not worthy. They are merely using the principles of the Universe; you can do the same, by engaging the power of intention.

Letting Go

Journal

When did you act against your inner voice telling you to do something?

What was the result?

Who in your world is not supporting your intentions?

How is it serving you to play small – what part of your ego/personality/fears are you protecting?

Earlier, I stated that non-attachment is a Universal Law. This principle applies equally to your intentions. Set them. Do what is necessary to support them. But don't obsess and worry about them, forever wondering when they will come about. Remember that worry, fear, and obsession are all lower order energies that will detract from or slow down the arrival of your success. Set your intentions, let them go, and go about your work as if the manifestation of your intention is just around the corner – which indeed it is!

Key Learnings:

- ✓ Setting an intention means invoking an interaction with the creative and intentional energies inherent in the Universe.
- ✓ The role of intention is to connect your business decisions or plans, to the means of having them manifest into something tangible.

- ✓ There is no substitute for working hard to develop your skills. You must be on your A game!
- ✓ Maintain your professionalism and integrity, and do no harm to others.
- ✓ If you are not getting what you want, then change your approach. Set your intention, and raise your energy to one that is confident, self-assured, and strong
- ✓ Set your intention, and then let it go!

#2: Attention

Your second business ally is attention. You will recognise attention when you experience qualities such as intuition, focus, discernment, detachment, release, non-judgment, courage, choice, accountability, curiosity, inspiration, and wisdom. Attention involves your noticing or paying heed to the existence of and proper alignment of those things, situations, people, events, or qualities that will bring your intentions into being – as well as being attentive to the elimination or relegation of things that will interfere with the manifestation of your intentions. Just as you would agree your strategy, and be attentive to the steps you would take with a human business partner, now you're having a real-time conversation with spirit, and doing exactly the same thing. As with intention, there's no heavy lifting required, as you can only pay attention in the present moment. But when you do, you will notice the organising principle at work – bringing about that which you set your intention upon.

Believe in Your Intuition

Paying attention also means engaging your intuition and being observant. **True story:** Chip Conley, hotelier and former CEO of Joie de Vivre Hospitality, a chain of some 50 hotels in the San Francisco Bay area, learned to pay attention only after a series of disastrous events. When hit by a cataclysmic combination of the dot com crash, the Iraq war, a major virus outbreak (SARS), 9/11, and the Afghan war, his hotels suffered a 35% drop in revenue. Facing potential failure, he turned to his roots as a Stanford business student, and wandered into a bookstore looking for a business book that would inspire him. Instead, he stumbled upon psychologist Abraham Maslow's work. Curiosity led him to wonder about the application of Maslow's principles to business, and whether those principles could turn his company around. It worked! By employing austerity measures, along with theories based upon Maslow's Hierarchy of Needs, he avoided laying off any of his 1000 employees, and resuscitated his business – which became the 2nd largest boutique hotel operator in the US.

> **Activity B:** Set your intention upon the successful outcome of your endeavours. Through the power of your active imagination, see yourself joyfully fulfilling your business vision, and know with certainty that your goal is on its way to you. Release your intention to the power of the Universe and don't get too wrapped up in all the details; know they will get worked out over time. And for goodness sake, don't spend time trying to convince people who are not positively supporting your ideas (that does not include people who are offering constructive criticism, of course, and trust your instincts to tell you the difference). After all, what's the point? Trying to convince them is keeping you at the level of your ego. The Universe already knows your positive intentions, and is cooperating with you to bring about the resources and persons you need. If anyone currently in your world doesn't fit with your vision of success, bless him or her with positive thoughts, thank them, and move along. Soon enough your manifested vision will fill your world and occupy your time, and the naysayers will be a distant, hopefully fond, memory.

So, how did Conley do this? By paying attention, by engaging his curiosity, by being willing to suspend judgment, and by following his intuition, he realised that people who stayed at his various hotels did so for the experience. Conley designed his hotels to be mirrors for the aspirations of his customers, creating "identity refreshments" as he termed them. Using the famous psychologist's theories, he learned to create peak experiences, not only for customers but for his employees and investors too, ultimately creating a peak experience for the entire organisation.

That's the power of engaging attention. In practice, it means being fully behind your intentions, being alert to the signals that are all around you – all of which are giving the nod towards the things you've asked for, the things you are manifesting right now. These signals are also alerting you to the many valuable ideas contained in this book – and which ones you should implement right away! Ignore or marginalise your doubts and fears, and remain in faithful alignment with your intentions, by thinking and doing what you need to do. Like Chip Conley and other successful business proprietors, you must persevere. Do not stop until you achieve the objects of your intentions.

Sometimes, the mental recordings of your experiences which run in the subconscious, just outside of the awareness of the conscious mind, can derail your focus. Because they're outside of your conscious mind, you're not aware of them. But they're there, causing havoc, sending unconscious signals to the Universal Field. Recall the course participant I spoke about earlier, the one with the negative thoughts about money. She was unaware of the source of those thoughts at the conscious level, and without that awareness, her thoughts were adversely affecting her intentions and ability to see and grasp opportunities. As a result, she was failing to make the changes she yearned for.

This is where I believe a coach or mentor can add genuine value. I've benefitted from several business coaches in my life, two in particular. One was a spiritual coach, the other a marketing coach. I credit both for aiding my awareness and consequently my growth in specific areas.

Journal

What thoughts of unworthiness, un-deservingness, guilt, pride, or shame do you secretly hold?

Are you ready to release them?

If you knew for sure that they were stopping your business from developing into a thriving one, would you be willing to release them now?

What is stopping you from asking for outside assistance?

Commit today to make spirit your source.

There are times when you just need help. Help to see the forest for the trees, help to keep you focused. Perhaps a part of being focused, for you, is recognising that you need help. If so, seek out the help you need. Intend it, surrender your ego to your spiritual business partner (your source), be attentive to the signals that tell you that you are on the right path, and then permit your help to come through in perfect fashion for you.

Making Spirit Your Source

You might have already considered hiring a coach. However, it's common to put this off, with excuses such as, 'I don't have the money' or 'This would never really work for me.' By now, you should be realising that stories such as these are just illusions. All of the resources that you need to manifest your intentions will come from the same source – you need only step into your intention and focus upon it. In 2005, I invited Iyanla Vanzant, a coach whose work I greatly admire, to Jamaica to help us celebrate my firm's anniversary. During one of our inspiring conversations, focused specifically on money, I recall her saying, 'Spirit is my source.' I've never forgotten these words.

Only you can determine how many times you want to go around and around with the same story, getting the same results that you don't like, before taking the steps necessary to change the story with a different intention and applied attention. When you do, however, you'll wonder why it took you so long.

Key Learnings: Attention involves noticing or paying attention to the existence and proper alignment of the things, situations, people, events, or qualities, that will bring your intentions into being.

- ✓ Engage your intuition and be observant.
- ✓ Engage your curiosity and suspend judgment.
- ✓ Work to eliminate or relegate things, people, ideas, or beliefs that will interfere with the manifestation of your intentions.
- ✓ Exercise persistence.
- ✓ Don't be afraid to seek out appropriate help.
- ✓ Make Spirit your ultimate source.

#3: Love

Your third business ally is love. Love vibrates in expressions of passion, compassion, non-judgment, gratitude, kindness, joy, beauty, truth, patience, courage, and forgiveness. If spirit is your source, love is the energy that powers your source, and no strategy will bring you lasting success without it. If you've ever tried meditation, then you might have experienced a rare type of joy, where all your thoughts disappear, replaced by an overwhelming feeling of oneness with spirit. When you experience this for the first time, there will be no doubt in your mind that pure love powers the Universal Field.

Demonstrating Love in Business

True story: When Jamaica Money Market Brokers (a Jamaican financial institution) opened their doors for business in 1992, declaring love as their motivating force – their raison d'etre – and used the word 'love' liberally in their marketing and advertising, it's fair to say that they raised a few eyebrows. After all, financial institutions are usually characterised by stoicism and logical left-brain activity, not sloppy emotionalism. But this never stopped Jamaica Money Market Brokers. Today, and hundreds of thousands of clients later, the business has firmly established itself as a financial powerhouse in the Caribbean. They have demonstrated dramatically that intellectual capacity **and** love together can elevate and sustain a business, no matter its type.

You too can demonstrate love in your business, in many ways. Like my fellow author Ruby McGuire, my law firm incorporates giving to our community as a way of expressing love, although as she explains, there are many ways of doing it. We seem to resonate with teenagers; our firm is actively involved with two projects for teenagers, one for girls and the other for boys. Most, if not all of our team members are directly involved in one way or another, and while the activities we do with these young people couldn't be further from the practice of law, there's no doubt that the members of my team benefit personally and directly from the engagement. The young people are delighted, and so are we.

Just like lower energies expressed as fear, deceit, or spite, love also operates in a loop. All energy attracts its own kind, which ultimately reverberates back to you. When you give love, it will come right back to you in some form or another. It may or may not come from the same place or person to which you gave it, but come it will – provided that when you give love, you do so unconditionally, without strings attached.

It is important to give love to everything that you do, and to everyone that you encounter, including the naysayers you encounter on your journey to success. Give love to every single one of your clients – even the ones that you claim are difficult! And, if you find a particular client difficult, use this as an opportunity to demonstrate a different expression of love – forgiveness or gratitude. Gratitude, for instance, has a way of dissolving minor irritations and raising the energy of a negative situation. It can be a powerful aid to your healing when practised regularly.

Giving Love to Yourself Is Just as Important

> **Journal**
>
> In what circumstances and around whom do you feel your heart centre close?
>
> Does your heart need to heal?
>
> How can you implement heart centredness in your business?
>
> How can you show love to your clients?

On the topic of personal healing, permit me to address something that I see quite commonly. During the early period of business development, it may take a while, years possibly, for the fruits of your work to manifest. It is during this time that you are required to hold faith and to truly love yourself, as you express patience. But it can be challenging. I recall a conversation with a CEO who said that she wouldn't think much of a lawyer driving an old car; I assume she defines a lawyer's success by the outward material expressions he or she owns. I told her that I thought this was unfortunate, for two main reasons. Firstly, it does take time for one's good to arrive, and patience is a virtue that should be encouraged and admired. But more importantly, material possessions are no measure of competence. I informed her that she might be missing out on the skills of an extremely capable lawyer (and here you could replace "lawyer" with coach or other business proprietor), one who has negligible outward signs of success merely because he or she chooses to donate much of their disposable wealth to charity!

You may experience similar challenges while you wait for your business to grow. The way through such periods is via the demonstration of love. This time though, it's about giving love to yourself. Be as extravagant with yourself as your pocket can afford. I had an old Toyota Corolla when I first started out, and frankly, I was happy for it – when it wasn't in the repair shop that is! I probably had one good suit to begin with as well. But as my means grew, I slowly added to my collection of good suits. Your thing may be jewellery, or a tiny apartment nicely decorated. Or, you may have little interest in material possessions. Frankly, it doesn't matter. Spirit doesn't care. Spirit is defined in and through love, so when you feel judged by someone, including yourself, remind yourself that you are here to share your gifts and demonstrate love. Put the energy of love into your craft, into your clients, your colleagues, and your community. Love is always the way. When you show love, the Universal Field gives you love back.

Love energy is responsible for the growing consciousness in the business sector, in the conscious capitalism movement, the conscious lawyer movement, the conscious leadership movement, and in many other movements too. In each of these movements, higher purpose and not profit is deemed more important, and businesspeople and leaders are searching for ways to offer meaning to their clients and employees. Companies such as Whole Foods Market®, South West Airlines, Ben & Jerry's, and others, are leading the way in demonstrating that win-win solutions serve humanity over win-lose solutions – a strategy that is borne from love.

Key Learnings:

- ✓ Love is the energy that powers your source.
- ✓ Love your work, love your clients, see beauty in your circumstances until your intentions manifest the new and higher vision you have for yourself.
- ✓ Through your passion, enthusiasm, and desire to serve, love will magnify itself in all the areas of your life.
- ✓ The way through difficult periods of your business is through the demonstration of love in patience and self-care.
- ✓ Love is always the way. When you show love, the Universal Spirit gives you love back.

Summary

I have shared with you my business strategy, which is a simple one. Search for your spiritual business partner (your higher self). Ensure that you get to know your partner's attributes, through the attainment of consciousness and the practise of presence. Align to your soul's purpose with what brings meaning to you. Then, support your co-created vision with a robust management team comprised of the powerful trio: intention, attention, and love.

By now, you will have realised that your partner and management team are all you, operating at maximum capacity and in line with the expansive Universal Laws of the Cosmos! When integrated, they represent a richly talented, gifted, and creative you, and they work together in harmony for your success!

Remember, clients are attracted to who you are. The more work you do on clarifying, growing and expressing your inner self, the more you will see this reflected in the people who will reach out to you to help them. As you become proficient at using the Universal Laws, your clients will find you. Recently, in a conversation with a very successful coaching colleague, we shared that neither of us overtly advertise our respective businesses or canvass for work that much anymore. Indeed, nearly 100% of our clients are from referrals, either from existing clients or from others who know of our work. Success has a way of advertising itself.

The manifestations of prosperity and success in your business are reflections of your inner work. They are the gifts of spirit that keep on giving from an abundant source when you apply the principles. They don't work for some people and not others. It doesn't even matter if you think it is all mumbo jumbo; they will work whether you believe them or not. They are the laws of the Universe, and they work for all of us.

Share your success stories with me; I'd love to hear them. Contact me via the email addresses on the next page.

Biography

Lorna Phillips is a successful commercial lawyer, social enterprise entrepreneur, Accredited Master Coach, trainer, and author. She specialises in crafting unique governance solutions for organisations undergoing transformation, whether through expansion, business succession, or re-organisation.

Lorna is managing partner of award-winning law firm Nicholson Phillips, Attorneys-at-Law, and founder of the Centre for Original Governance. She brings over thirty-five years of combined legal and coaching experience in helping individuals and organisations align for success through the crafting and implementing of integrated legal solutions. Lorna is married and lives with her husband and teenage son in Jamaica.

lorna@nicholsonphillips.com or contactCFOG@gmail.com

[i] Freedom Lights Our World (FLOW) Inc., and organisation co-founded by John Mackey, CEO of Whole Foods Market and Michael Strong. FLOW is about liberating the human spirit for good and is dedicated to the big idea that creative entrepreneurs can help solve all the challenges in the world. They offer public programmes which provide a point of entry into social enterprise and opportunities for action. You can access information from www.flowidealism.org.

[ii] 'Be the Solution – How Entrepreneurs and Conscious Capitalists Can Solve All the World's Problems', Michael Strong,

[iii] Be the Solution", Chapter 6 Business As Service – Doing Well to Do Good, p. 125

CHAPTER THREE

By

Ali Temple

The Mind Game

For many years I performed all over the world as a professional acrobat. Since then, I have gone on to build a successful business as a Performance Coach, helping people get exceptional results in all areas of their personal life and business. Training and performing as an acrobat was the greatest educator in how to overcome fear and learn the power of process. It also taught me how essential it is to refine your skills, as well as how to be successful in a hugely competitive industry. My unique experience is part of what guides me as a coach. What I write about here comes from a place of knowing, based on a relentless, and at times obsessive, pursuit of success.

In my chapter I will give you an honest and direct approach to what I know works. Using both my personal experience, and my experience of coaching others to overcome massive challenges, I want to help you improve your mindset, and take action that will make a difference in your life (or business).

Mindset is a huge topic, and for me it's one of the most important. You can have all the best knowledge and skills in the world, but if you lack the mindset to implement them, then you're never fully prepared to succeed. So much of what you'll have to navigate as a solopreneur will require you to have excellent mental agility and discipline. I want to see to it that you get it right, and proceed with the very best toolkit for how to win the mind game. Together, we can help you to keep taking the action that is essential to your success.

Of the many areas of mindset, I'm going to focus on the three key areas that I believe will make the most difference to you. This will ensure you are mentally equipped, with a mindset that will allow you to act and get results in your business. These areas will be:

- Motivation.
- Dealing with fear, failure, and rejection.
- Standing out from the crowd.

Before we proceed with those topics, I want you to ask yourself an incredibly important question. This is one that I believe every successful person ultimately has to ask themselves at some point, in order to take the next steps to greatness. And the question is this: 'What does success mean to you?'

Success

Success is a word that gets thrown around a lot in the world of business. But what does it mean? The way we speak about it often indicates that most people are waiting to be successful: 'I'll be successful when...' 'What will make you successful is...' Some people might even consider themselves unsuccessful, until that time arrives. If you tend to think this way, it can have a detrimental, even intimidating, impact on your mindset, and it can cause you to feel that you're already unsuccessful before you've even started. You might feel incapable of bridging the gap between yourself and so-called successful people. Moving forward, I want to invite you to think of success as **effectiveness**. Rather than asking, 'How successful am I?' ask yourself, 'How effective am I?' There are so many things that you can be effective at, from achieving a desired outcome to turning an idea into action and getting results – building a business isn't about taking one single, massive, world-beating action. It's lots of small things done well and consistently, over a long period of time, that are effective in driving you towards achieving your goals. By being effective, you are being successful on a daily basis.

The other area of success that you need to consider, is how you define the term. People create huge amounts of pain and frustration for themselves, by comparing their own success with other people's definition of it. It is essential that you define what success means to you personally – your vision of success on your terms. Not what Instagram or YouTube tells you it looks like, but what you want for your own life and business. This might be a sales figure, monthly income, work-life balance, financial freedom, being able to provide for someone, or a certain lifestyle. Whatever it is you want, you need to have absolute clarity about what that is. After all, how do you hit the target if you don't know where it is? Often when we're stuck, there's nothing wrong with the goal, it's down to a lack of clarity about exactly what we're trying to do. This is about knowing your end goal, so that all actions funnel you towards it – meaning your actions are aligned, keeping you on track, and producing tangible results.

It's easy to think of success as money, cars, and houses, or simply making loads of sales and generating a huge income. If that's what you want, that's great. However, what you need to do is define the success you want, and then understand what it will give you and why that's important in your life. For instance, financial freedom is one of my main goals right now. However, that's simply not detailed enough. I also need an actual specific number to aim for, otherwise how do I know if I'm achieving it or not? So, I set my end number, then chunk back from there, plotting where I need to be and by when, laying out a path before me. Financial freedom isn't just for the sake of the number, but for what the number represents. For me, money doesn't equal happiness or make me a better person in any way. For me, money equals freedom. More money equals more options: for travel, adventure, spontaneity, and looking after my family. That's powerful to me. What is powerful for you?

You need to find a vision of success that will genuinely fulfil you. Tony Robbins says, 'Success without fulfilment is the ultimate failure.' What does that mean? Well, have you ever worked your ass off for something you really wanted, only to feel an unforeseen sense of emptiness upon achieving it? That's success without fulfilment, and the emptiness is caused by your goal not fulfilling one of your values. I've seen this many times with clients who have everything, yet are still unhappy and stressed. Do not do that to yourself. You must make sure your vision is in alignment with your values, and that you have a purpose that truly fulfils you.

Exercise: Reframing Success

- **Q** What do you want/need to be effective at, as the business owner?
- **Q** What do you want to be great at?
- **Q** What is **your** vision of success?
- **Q** What does it mean to you?
- **Q** What will it allow you to do?

Now that you're clearer on what it is you're trying to achieve, you will be able to apply the knowledge and techniques in the book in a much more focused, specific, and effective way, meaning you'll get far better results.

Key Learnings:

- Swap *Successful*, for *Effective.*
- Pursue your own vision of success!
- All action should take you towards your goal, otherwise it's taking you away from it.
- Understand exactly what your success will give you, and why that's meaningful to you.
- Remember, success without fulfilment equals failure.

Motivation - The Driving Force Behind Our Actions

Understanding the mechanics behind motivation is essential. Once you learn to understand this, you'll have access to one of the key tools of success, which is the ability to act. Your journey as a solopreneur is going to be challenging, lonely, and frustrating at times. It will require huge amounts of time and effort to build your business, and you will be required to motivate yourself along the way. As a result, you must know how to generate motivation from within. The good news is, by anticipating and accepting these challenges as part of the process, you can deal with them far more effectively than if you are surprised by them – which many people are.

Motivation is an area with some misconceptions, so let's start right away by dismissing one of these – no one is motivated all the time! You can, however, develop your understanding of what influences your motivation, what causes it to waver, and, more importantly, how you can increase it. You need a proactive, consistent, and predictable way to get into a state that allows you to operate effectively. Notice I'm using the word **effective** now.

So, what is it that will truly motivate you? The answer is your **reason.** The reason behind your goals is the powerhouse that drives your action. If you want to achieve great things in any area of life, you will need a reason so compelling that it commands action, whether you are in the mood or not. You need a powerful and fulfilling reason, that will surpass all distractions and excuses. That's a huge difference between those who are successful and those who are not. Successful people act consistently, because they know why they're doing what they're doing. Unsuccessful people act only when they feel like it.

The reality is that motivation gets you started, but it's discipline that keeps you going. Discipline means forming positive and beneficial habits that facilitate progress towards your goal, then implementing those habits regardless of external factors or conditions – whether they are morning routines, working out, meditation or affirmations, structuring your time a certain way, weekly reviews, effective planning, an accountability partner, time management, working with a coach, or the rules you set yourself. Once you are motivated by a compelling reason, it's then about identifying the habits you need to stick to, even when you can't be bothered or lose your motivation. Think of this like going to the gym and working out. It doesn't matter if you want to exercise, or if you enjoy exercise; the physiological response is the same – you get stronger and fitter. The same is true of your daily disciplines. What often holds people up is that they are so focused on what they **want** to do rather than doing what they **need** to do. Therefore, you must constantly evaluate your actions to establish if they are helping or hindering you.

Implementing this level of discipline, even in the absence of motivation, is essential. In life and business, action is the currency of progress. When we experience progress, it builds excitement, confidence, results, momentum, and best of all creates motivation. I believe we are growth driven beings – we are rewarded by development. It's not always success that makes us happy, but the sense of moving forward in some way. That's because progress equals growth, which often equals happiness. Nature has seen to it that we are rewarded with a dump of feel good chemicals, such as endorphins, oxytocin, serotonin, and dopamine, as a way of encouraging us to do things where we grow or learn. It's the same buzz we get when we've exercised. It's nature's way of saying to do more of the things it knows are good for us. This is the sense of forward momentum that you are looking for in your business, to both create and sustain motivation. It's like waiting until you're fit, before you go to the gym. You can't wait until you're motivated to act. If you wait, you might never start. Action will feed the fire of your motivation, not the other way around.

A big challenge with motivation is that it's common to want everything now. This is because of the instant gratification, quick-fix, super-fast culture we have. When people don't get the immediate results they want, they lose interest, get discouraged, or take it as a sign that they can't do it. The issue is that most people's thinking is too short-term. The key skill of a successful and effective business owner, is to understand that it's not about the effect of an action made once or twice, but to know the compound effect of taking specific action consistently over a long period of time. You don't need to be motivated all the time to act and get great results. If your vision is clear and you know your reason, then that will allow you to identify the action that is required. Your focus then needs to be about consistency, until you achieve the result you're aiming for. This has worked for me for years. Not because I'm always motivated, but because I apply the discipline and the power of process that allows me to take consistent action that will generate results. So, rather than asking, 'What do I need to do to get motivated?' I instead ask, 'What's the reason I'm doing this?' or 'What habits do I need to implement to keep me moving forward?' When the answer becomes clear, I get on with it and create forward momentum.

If you are to be successful, then you must know what drives you and how to sustain that in the tough times – for there will be plenty. When you get demotivated you can feel stuck, frustrated, or overwhelmed. You might even start to question your mission, yourself, and your ability. Here are some of the common reasons for losing motivation:

- Slow progress.
- Lack of clarity.
- Lack of results.
- Failure(s).

- Rejection.
- Lack of acknowledgement from others.
- Comparing yourself to others.
- Burnout.
- Loneliness on the entrepreneurial journey.
- Reality not living up to your expectations.
- Lack of variety.
- Too much risk.
- Stress.
- Lack of knowledge.
- Focusing on problems rather than opportunities.
- Lack of fun or enjoyment.
- Goal(s) not being in alignment with values.
- Focusing on a short-term rather than long-term picture.
- Unwillingness to do the level of work required.
- Not actually wanting it enough.

Here's what will motivate you:

- Your reason.
- Goal(s) in alignment with values.
- Taking action.
- Taking ownership.
- Experiencing progress.
- Results.
- Having fun.
- Contributing to other people's happiness.
- Adding value.
- Solving problems.
- Experiencing personal growth.
- Reporting back to a coach or accountability partner.

Willingness

How much you really want it, will influence your motivation in a big way. A lot of the time people say that they want something, but the reality is that they're only really expressing an interest in it. When people find out the volume of work it requires to make whatever it is happen, their interest tapers off. As a performance coach, I make it a point to question clients on their level of desire about their goals, in order to assess their commitment. This isn't to be provocative; I do it to help expose even the tiniest amount of doubt or lack of willingness. When we truly and deeply want to achieve something, because we know with certainty it will bring genuine fulfilment, then we are motivated to keep pushing through, no matter what. If we're not, then we'll eventually find excuses and give up. If this means that you or clients choose to let go of a goal, then good. It means you're not going to waste your valuable time or energy pursuing something that was going to be given up on at some point anyway, which would only make you feel deflated and negative about yourself. Letting go of the ideas and goals that genuinely aren't right for you, means you can prioritise the better more fulfilling ones. If you are to be truly motivated in a sustainable way, you must be absolutely committed to your goal. No matter what.

The world is full of amazing potential, technology, medical breakthroughs, and achievements. From the internet to space travel, feats of extreme human performance to financial success, behind every skill, passion, or hobby there is someone finding a way to monetise it. Within context, we can achieve almost anything we can imagine. So, it's not a question of whether you'll be successful or not. The real question is, how willing are you? Everybody wants to be successful, but fewer are prepared to take the level of action that it requires. The problem might not be that you've lost motivation; it might be that you're not willing to do what is required to achieve the next step of the process. If your reason doesn't justify the means, that's when you start to lose interest and become inactive. Before you go any further, the most important question I can ask you is: 'How willing are you to do everything it takes to achieve your goal?'

A lack of motivation is perhaps one of the biggest enemies of progress to business owners. If your motivation wavers at times, you're not alone. It happens to everyone at some point. While it may have slowed you down in the past, you can change that now, because you have the right information. Focus on your vision, the reason that matters to you, and what daily disciplines you must implement to make it happen. By doing these you'll inevitably experience progress, which you'll then feel great about. In turn, this will show you that you can do this, and you'll be even more motivated to take more action.

Key Learnings:

- ✓ Know your compelling reason.
- ✓ If your reason isn't big enough, your excuses will be.
- ✓ Motivation gets you started, but it's discipline that keeps you going.
- ✓ Daily disciplines keep you on track and ensure progress.
- ✓ Implementing positive habits creates progress that inspires motivation.
- ✓ Action is the currency of progress.
- ✓ Chart your progress.
- ✓ Consider the compound effect of both actions and habits.
- ✓ How willing you are, will determine how much action and progress you achieve in your goals.

Exercise: Willingness Appraisal

- **Q** What are your goals?
- **Q** What will you **realistically** have to do to achieve them?
- **Q** How willing are you to do everything it takes, to achieve what's on that list?
- **Q** What are you unwilling to do?

Fear, Failure and Rejection

"Fear killed more dreams that failure ever did." – Suzy Kassem

I have witnessed so many extremely capable and highly skilled people fail to achieve their goals because of fear. Fear is a debilitating force, that clouds judgment, casts shadows over self-belief, and limits the amount of action people take. Few things have such a detrimental effect on your business. If you are to become all that you want to be, successful on your own terms, and with the business that you want, then you absolutely must unshackle yourself from the burden of this mindset.

The most common reasons for not doing the things we want are **fear of failure**, **fear of judgment,** and **fear of rejection.** We're afraid that our ideas won't work, that no one will book us, buy from us, or use our services. Equally, we worry about what people think of us. If you want to move forward confidently and effectively, you need to know how to deal with your natural fears around rejection, judgment and failure. Then, most importantly, let them go.

Rejection

Put simply, fear of rejection often stops people even trying. The way business owners often enact this is when trying to get new clients, networking, or making a sale. They interpret someone saying 'No' as failure, so subconsciously try to protect themselves from rejection, with the fatal mistake of not even reaching out, asking, sending the email, or making the call. Business owners tell themselves that customers won't want their service, that it's rude to ask for the sale, or that the idea would never work in the first place. And in doing this, they make the fatal mistake of making the client's decision for them. All those things are the voice of fear – the fear that you might not be good enough.

How confident are you that you can genuinely and effectively help your clients? If you know you can help them, and you're committed to making your business work, then it's your obligation to reach out, offer and ask, then follow up and ask again. You have two very simple jobs:

1. Be great at what you do.
2. Offer what you can do, to people you can help.

It is not your job to make the decision for potential clients on whether they want your service or not. Talking yourself out of offering your services will completely stop you in your tracks. It's a negative and deeply limiting mindset, which will result in slower progress – limiting your results, destroying your confidence, and making you even less likely to reach out in future.

When I moved to London to perform, one of the key skills that helped make me successful wasn't even anything to do with my physical ability. I would go online and compile a list of every single person I could find in the industry that might even be slightly likely to book performers, such as agents, producers, directors, choreographers, theatres, and film studios. Sometimes I would send over a hundred emails a week offering my services, sharing my pictures and showreels, and letting people know who I was and what I could do. I used to post info packs with a DVD showreel, pictures, CV, and business card to their address too. This was before YouTube, and at the time hustling like this was not common practice with performers. When some of my peers heard about this, they laughed in my face. Well, who's laughing now? I had a relentless and tenacious approach to self-promotion, because I understood that it was up to me to let people know what I do and how I can help them. At the start, I was largely ignored. If I was lucky, I would get 5 replies out of 100. I considered that a good week. But the main point is, I didn't give up. I kept trying, and now you need to do the same. Be tenacious and unyielding in your efforts to put yourself out there, and let people know what you do and how you can help them.

With consistency, my numbers grew. I started etching my name into the mind of agents across the UK. When events came in, I knew they would be looking for performers, and it was my mission to put my name at the top of their list. Gradually, over time, I got more bookings. With more gigs I got more recommendations, as word got around about my skillset and work ethic. It got to the stage where I was being directly booked to perform on the biggest jobs in the industry around the world, while everyone else had to queue up to audition and compete. I applied the exact same principles to my coaching business when I set that up too, and in the first year of coaching I was speaking at events, selling out my own workshops, and coaching clients in several countries around the world – simply because I don't make clients' minds up for them. I reach out, and ask and offer, knowing that if someone says 'No' then it doesn't mean that I'm no good – it just means they don't yet know me enough, that I've not communicated what I do effectively enough, or that they don't see the value in working with me, yet.

So, pick up your phone, get on the email, propose ideas, make suggestions, introduce yourself to people, tell them what you do, solve problems, and add value. Embrace every opportunity you encounter, and put your ideas into action. The return on nothing is zero. Read that again: you will get nothing back if you don't try. If you reach out and make offers consistently, then the sheer law of averages dictates that you will increase your client base. This will also help you develop your promotional skills and boost your confidence.

Exercise

- **Q** If you were to implement this mindset, what would you do differently?
- **Q** What action could you take right now to reach out, offer, follow up, and action your idea?
- **Q** What could the effect of that be?
- **Q** How would it help your business?

Judgement

So many people shrink themselves and shy away from their true calling, ignoring their own purpose, because they're worried about what someone else might think. Even I haven't been immune to this. I'm driven, proactive, motivated, and after living the last 15 years of my life on stage have little issue with drawing attention to myself. Yet it took me almost a full year of inner struggle just to start posting Facebook videos of coaching content. *'Who's he to tell people how to live their life? What does he know about it? He's just an acrobat, what would he know?!'* This was the voice of my inner demon. So, month after month, I didn't share any of the knowledge, information, or skills I had with others. In doing so I never helped a single person, never built a following, never demonstrated my unique ability, never let people get to know me, never solved any problems for anyone, never gave anyone hope, encouragement, or positivity, never gave anyone a new perspective on their life, mindset, or business. All because I was worried about what other people would think. And that wasn't even the worst part. When we stifle our true inner voice like this, it's spiritual suicide – which is the direct path to dissatisfaction and unhappiness. I was focusing on other people who I either didn't know or, truthfully, didn't even respect anyway, and it was stopping me from pursuing my goal.

Where your focus needs to be, is on you – on refining your skills and bringing real value to those you can help. Not on fear, doubt, or negativity. I can't emphasise strongly enough how detrimental it is to do what I did, to yourself. I've been fortunate, in that I've found a way to follow my own path. Moving to London with a powerful vision of being a highly successful performer was pure instinct, and I pursued this obsessively. Then, when I felt a new calling to study as a Life and Business Coach, I took the necessary action – having no real idea how it would work, but I knew it was something I was being called towards. It was an education that finally gave me the vocabulary I needed to communicate a lifetime of lessons and experiences, that I knew could make a huge difference to others. None of the thousands of live performances I've experienced all over the world, or all the clients I've helped, would have been possible if I let the fear of what others thought dictate these life-defining decisions. It's been far from easy, and sometimes it's nearly broken me – taking the path less travelled. However, the richness and variety of unbelievable experiences I've had has been so fulfilling and empowering.

When you take bold action – action that is truly right for you – it teaches you that you have the ability to do anything in life. It will build confidence, resilience, self-esteem, and give you a mindset that allows you to tackle any challenge in your life, because you have the facility to do so and are in control of your direction. You are capable, with the right mindset and the skills laid out here, in the pages of this book.

Often, the path of a solopreneur means going against the conditioning of most of your educational life, where you have been very deliberately trained to become an employee. It's not that there's a problem with your ability to be successful, it's that we're pack animals, and we're programmed with a fear that makes us not want to step outside the agreed and normal parameters of our group.

There is no substitute for the power that comes with letting go of fear, and acknowledging the truth, which is this: it doesn't matter what others think of your dreams and goals. Real freedom is the absence of fear. There are already enough obstacles on the path to success, without you being one too. You must remove yourself as the barrier to your own progress. Be your own biggest supporter and cheerleader, the champion of your own story. When you begin to truly act in accordance with your purpose, nothing will feel more empowering!

Exercise: Limiting Beliefs

- **Q** What is the fear or belief that's been holding you back?
- **Q** What's been the effect of that fear/thought?
- **Q** What specifically do you need to let go of, or reframe?
- **Q** What is your new empowering mindset, that will allow you to make confident and bold decisions?

Failure

If you want to be truly and consistently successful, then you must build a tolerance for failure and rejection. You must change your relationship with these elements, and understand that they are a natural, inevitable, and essential part of the process of learning and growth. My own philosophy was that 99% of success was failure.

How many times would you let a child try to walk before you told them that maybe walking just isn't for them? You wouldn't, obviously. You'd allow them to try as many times as it takes, until they could do it. So, what's the reason this changes as adults? Why do we decide that if something doesn't work at the first or second attempt, then it means we can't do it and we've failed? We then associate failure with our identity, with who we are. We take it to mean that if we're unsuccessful, that means we are not good enough in some way, not smart enough, not skilled enough, not experienced enough, not knowledgeable enough, not rich enough, not popular enough, not cool enough, not likeable enough, not confident enough – so we won't ever be able to do it, so we should therefore give up our idea, because our business will never work. But is that really what it means?

The way to get around this is to change both your perception and definition of failure, and then develop a new philosophy that redefines what it means. You need to develop a growth mindset, over a success or failure mindset. Being unsuccessful doesn't make you a failure. I'd suggest that not learning from it, or not trying again, is equal to failure. When you look back at all the things in life that you were unsuccessful at, or that you labelled as a failure, and view them with total honesty, you may note that in many cases you never failed – you made the decision to give up. It's important to distinguish the difference. Could you have tried again? Tried something else? Got help? Tried a little harder? Been more disciplined? If you are unsuccessful, it doesn't mean you are failing. It simply means that you don't have the right knowledge, skills, information, or the right way…yet! So, when something doesn't go to plan, you need to divorce yourself from the negative reaction to it, and identify the opportunities for learning. Then, go again, and implement these lessons the next time round. As an acrobat, I looked at practise as controlled failure. I played at the edge of my ability, continually drilling new moves to refine my skills. This meant falling and failing for hours on end, every day. This is what practise is.

Training in acrobatics involves a huge amount of repetition, gruelling physical conditioning, and confronting fears, working at heights, new aerial manoeuvres, and suffering from painful or career ending injuries. Launching myself into the air, knowing I might not be landing on my feet, is something I had to build a tolerance for. Sometimes, learning new acrobatics feels like you are physically and mentally leaping into darkness. You have to fly into the air sometimes with no real idea of where you are or what will happen, but you must trust in your instincts, skills, and conditioning that you will do the right thing. It's just the same in business. The difference is, however, that if and when I make a mistake with acrobatics, the consequences could be exponentially more painful than someone saying, 'No thanks,' or a few empty seats in a workshop. So, are you still telling me you can't reach out just a bit more?

I'm not being confrontational here. I'm giving you the power of perspective. It's not that I'm fearless; it's that I accept it as an appropriate response to the situation, but I know how important it is to act anyway. And to build the skill of feeling the fear and doing it anyway. It's about having the self-awareness to know what drives our fears and to overcome them. Do you not have the time, or are you worried about what a rejection means about your ability and who you think you are? Remember, courage isn't the absence of fear, but action in the face of it. The absolute last thing you want in your business is the feeling of regret. Not because you failed, but because you failed to get out of your own way and really try.

"The master has failed more times than the beginner has even tried." – Stephen McCranie

Key Learnings:

- ✓ Be tenacious in your approach.
- ✓ Don't make clients' decisions for them.
- ✓ 3 common fears holding us back: Fear of failure, fear of judgement, fear of rejection.
- ✓ Focus on you, your business, and the value you can bring to others.
- ✓ Redefine your definition of failure.
- ✓ Build your tolerance for failure and rejection.
- ✓ Its none of your business what other people think of the chances of your goals.
- ✓ Adopt a growth mindset.
- ✓ Unsuccessful attempts simply mean you don't have the right knowledge, skills, information or way…yet!
- ✓ We don't fail. We give up.

Exercise – Reviewing failure

- **Q** What worked well?
- **Q** What didn't work well?
- **Q** What was the reason for that?
- **Q** What was I trying to achieve?
- **Q** What did I achieve?
- **Q** What progress did I make?

Q What did I learn from this?

Q What skills do I need to improve/develop?

Q What will I do differently next time?

Q What will I do next?

Q When will I do that?

From Competitor to Leader

How do you stand out from the crowd in a busy or competitive marketplace, especially when you are fresh to market? This is a pressing question for all new business owners. Some people love the feeling of competition, and gain a lot from it. Others find this debilitating, and completely shy away from it, to the point that they refuse to participate. At the beginning of your new business, you must accept that there will be a certain level of competition. This comes with the territory. As I said previously, behind every skill, passion, or hobby there is someone finding a way to monetise. So, you need to be able to answer the question of why your client should work with you specifically. It's natural that you will feel the need to compete with those already established, as you research, explore, and develop your skills to find your place.

When I began in the entertainment industry, I was in a highly competitive state. I had to queue up and audition, like every other performer in town, and it was soul destroying. Firstly, I had to get invited to the audition in the first place, an achievement in itself! Then, once I was in there, I had to compete with the best of the industry. At the auditions I couldn't help but eyeball the competition to see what they were doing, watching how they moved and behaved, even noting what they were wearing; anything I could do to learn what they were doing that was allowing them to get booked. There were areas I was weaker and less experienced at, and I struggled massively with fear and confidence in these parts of the casting. Even so, I had to put my fear aside and make sure I put myself at the front, so I could at least be seen as trying my best. I learned two lessons from this. The first was that pushing yourself well out of your comfort zone is the best way to grow, learn, and develop. Over time, this is what will make you an expert. Secondly, I learned that if you try to stand side by side with someone and compete with them at what they're great at, it puts you in a weak and frustrating position.

Despite my lack of confidence in certain areas, there were other sections of the casting where I knew I was the expert, and that my skills were far superior. This gave me confidence, more energy, and a feeling of certainty that I was going to deliver even under the pressure of the audition. When you are doing the thing you are best at, it gives you the ability to act with confidence and allows you to stand front and centre. The lessons from this can be equally employed when building a successful business. There are areas where you must remain present and competent in the marketplace, regardless of whether you are strong in this area or not. However, you must seek out any and all opportunities to demonstrate your real skill, knowledge, and expertise, and go full out – firing on all cylinders when you do.

As I became more known in the industry, people learned that I was highly skilled at certain things. Once people started to know who I was and what I could do, when the time came most of the other performers would actually stand back, give me space, and let me showcase my specialist skills. They totally accepted that I owned that section of the audition, because I had demonstrated time and time again that I was unrivalled in my ability and the way in which I delivered it. Most gave me the floor, and didn't even bother joining in with that part, because they knew it would only make them look totally inadequate next to me. I had beaten the competition physically – on a skill level – but also mentally too. I wasn't competing anymore, I was dominating. The important point here is that I did that because I was doing what I was best at, and I'm the best at being me. The casting agents had no choice but to take notice and cast me, because the whole room had come to a halt to watch. So, what are you best at? What will you need to do, to give the market no choice but to take notice?

This whole experience taught me that when I am truly being myself, I am at my best and most successful. I'm also at my happiest. It seems obvious, but so many people don't do this, and as a result never unleash their unique ability on the world. The same can be the case for you. You have an experience and skillset that when combined with an empowered mind and exceptional work ethic, will allow you to win on your terms!

When it comes to standing out from the crowd or getting seen in a busy marketplace, most beginner or inexperienced business owners try and compete with, or even emulate, others. They do this by regurgitating other people's content, products, or material, which almost inevitably means they're going to lose. This is frustrating and disheartening for a solopreneur, and can easily trigger the gremlins in your head, telling you that you're no good at this. What it really means is that the leaders and influencers of today are being authentic to who they are, and working to their best skills and strengths. No one will ever be better at being you, than you. Being true to who **you** are is what will make you stand out in a world of lookalikes.

Exercise

- Who are **you** really?
- What are **you** great at?
- What's **your** unique experience and skills?
- What way do **you** want to build your business?
- What area do you want to dominate?

When I was able to answer the above questions, I felt a huge and powerful sense of expansion. It was as if I was moving into a space of my own in the industry, a place that I had carved out just for me. I have done the exact same things in my coaching business. This is important, because when you are competing for business you fall into a mindset of scarcity. You'll be fearful that there aren't enough clients to go around, and you'll start asking questions, such as, 'What if someone else takes my clients?', 'What are they doing?', 'How much are others charging?', 'What service or product are they selling, to whom, and in what area?' This will put you in a negative and reactive state. Again, your focus will be on others rather than on you and your business – where it needs to be. I'm not saying that you shouldn't be aware of the market; I am saying focus on you.

As soon as I realised exactly what **I** was about, what success meant for me, what I personally wanted to do, and the specific way I wanted to do it, I became free from the struggle of standing out from the crowd. The crowd became irrelevant, because it was no longer about competing. The goal was to be working on me, my business, and the way I wanted to do it – my personal and meaningful goals. It was then about achieving **my** vision of success. I went from having feelings of scarcity, to abundance. This is a far more positive and empowering state to be in.

What this comes down to is self-awareness. To stand out from the crowd, you must really know yourself, because it's your uniqueness that will set you apart. This includes your strengths, skills, weaknesses, and quirks. Figure out exactly what it is you do, your unique contribution to the market, and your own way of doing it. What will not help you stand out from the crowd, is trying to be another version of someone else. To achieve this, you have to keep asking questions about yourself and the service you offer. Those who are willing and able to do this will have a higher level of self-knowledge that will lead to success.

Self-awareness comes from truthful and accurate feedback from others, which you should continually invite. It also comes from having an honest and healthy dialogue with yourself. Being able to identify your real fears and where they come from, as well as being able to impartially assess your key skills and natural shortcomings, is crucial. The key word here is **impartial.** Self-assessment is not an invitation to berate yourself or focus on what you're not good at or can't do, but to learn and improve.

As a performer, my competitive nature first helped me achieve success on the scene, and then drove me past the competition to the top – where I really stood out. Oddly, once I achieved that and began to really focus on what I wanted to do, I moved away from any interest or desire to compete, and began actively avoiding it. I had established myself with an unrivalled skillset, experience, and a client base that continually flowed – to the point where I was regularly fully booked and turning down jobs. As that sunk in with me, the sense of competition gave way to a realisation that I was in a space of my own. It just simply wasn't possible for other performers to compete with me. With this, I was able to fully focus on myself, be grateful for what I had accomplished, and be happy for others when they were successful too, because I knew that their success didn't threaten my own in any way. This brought me great joy. This is about transcendence, from competitor to leader! For you to be successful, I invite you to embark on this journey too.

Refining Skills

If you want to stand out from the crowd, and this is something I consider myself an expert in, then it's my personal philosophy that you need to do two things – have an ongoing commitment to refining your skills, and have an exceptional work ethic. Above all else, what will make you stand out from the crowd (for all the right reasons) is the same thing that will make your business a success – mastering your craft. It's as simple as that, but unfortunately that answer isn't sexy, and doesn't sell as many courses. There are few people queuing up to pay for a training course that says "just work bloody hard!"

Many people who want to be solopreneurs are so focused on attention, likes, views, or shares, and trying to emulate those more successful than themselves, that they forget what makes the best business owners and influencers so effective and popular in the first place – which is that they spent years getting exceptionally good at what they do. They are masters of their craft. That's why they have 6-figure clients, not because they watched one webinar. As Eddie Cantor once said, 'It takes years to become an overnight success.'

The pain point for so many new business owners isn't a lack of clients, it's the lack of patience to allow the power of process to take place. The foundation of that process must be about skill. What will really make you stand out from the crowd, is being outstanding at what you do! People are looking for you to be the expert. They want someone to solve their problem or add value to what they're trying to do. They want to see that you have the knowledge, skills, and ability to do what you say you can do, as quickly and as effectively as possible. There are so many people who fake it until they make it, that the public can now sense a disingenuous sales pitch from a mile off. Skill and talent are universal. These qualities transcend all languages. When you establish yourself as the skilful expert, it gives clients certainty, and the assurance that you have what they need. They want to know that you can move them from where they are now to where they want to be. So, show them!

Not only will prioritising skill help you stand out, it also means you'll make more money. The more skilled you are, or the more knowledge you have, the more valuable you become. This means you will be able to develop a niche service or product. A specialist in any industry becomes more valued and more highly paid. Yes, getting public attention and using social media are super important, as these are valuable tools for your business. However, putting skills and knowledge at the forefront of your strategy will get you recognition and respect, that will drive your success forward in a way that you can monetise and build on. Whilst working as a performance coach, I have followed this exact philosophy, with a relentless commitment to learning and developing my skills, so that I can get better results for clients. I do this, because it works.

This strategy is so powerful, because it removes the limiting belief that you need to be perfect from the start. Anyone can become amazing at something, but only if you learn and practise effectively. There's so much free and easily accessible information out there, that it's never been so easy to learn. In the age of information, ignorance or a lack of knowledge is now a choice. This has been the superpower in my success – being a fanatical learner. I've never considered myself to be more naturally talented than anyone else. The reality is, I simply outwork people. The beautiful thing about hard work is that it requires no pre-existing skills, and costs nothing.

Key Learnings:

- ✓ To stand out from the crowd, be outstanding!
- ✓ Commit to refining your skills.
- ✓ Seek out opportunities to demonstrate your knowledge, skills, and expertise.
- ✓ Develop an exceptional work ethic.

- ✓ Master your craft.
- ✓ Seek to be known for skills, standards, knowledge, and quality.
- ✓ Having a higher skill level allows you to create a niche service, which equals being higher paid.
- ✓ Become a fanatical learner.
- ✓ Transcend from competitor to leader.

Exercise: Getting Clear

- **Q** What is your unique experience?
- **Q** What are you especially good at?
- **Q** Who do you need to be, in order to stand out from the crowd?
- **Q** How can you package your skills or experience, to offer something unique?
- **Q** What is it exactly that you give to clients?
- **Q** What's the way you want to run your business?
- **Q** What opportunities could you find to showcase your skill, knowledge, or expertise?
- **Q** What is it that you want to be a leader in?

What I've laid out here are some of the key philosophies and skills that will help you to think critically, with clarity and focus, develop your self-awareness, and take fearless action that will drive you forward. With this mindset, you will be able to take the vast amount of information in this book and implement it in a way that gets results. For me, that's what this is all about.

Above all else, what I really want to do is give you permission to trust yourself and follow your vision – to have a commitment to refining your skills, but not to discount your unique ability and experience. Embrace your uniqueness and nurture it. When you win the mind game, you'll find yourself in a place where you are capable of anything. The right mindset is the most powerful weapon in your armoury, and one that you are completely responsible for.

It's so easy to read as many business and personal development books as you can, and once finished, immediately move on to the next one. Rather than doing that with this book, I encourage you to re-read the whole book again, taking notes of all your key learning points, and completing all of the exercises. The exercises are there for a reason. It's not about how many books you read, or what the best one is. It's about what **you** can do with the information you've been given.

If you want to share with me what you have taken away from this chapter, such as your actions, mindset shift, progress, results, general feedback, or if there's a particular challenge I can help you with, then I'd love to hear from you.

Drop me an email at info@steadfast-coaching.com

Biography

Ali Temple is a former international acrobat, property investor entrepreneur, and performance coach. Having lost his father at the age of 14, and with declining mental health, he embarked on a personal development journey that would become a life obsession. Driven by an intense desire to help others, he chose to go on and train as a coach himself.

Ali has turned his greatest pain into his strongest asset, coaching others in need, with experience, wisdom, and intuition. He is now thankful to be able to coach people in various countries, helping people in both their personal lives and their business lives.

www.steadfast-coaching.com

CHAPTER FOUR

By

Anna M Stapleton

Your Pathway to Success

The purpose of this chapter is to emphasise the importance of the emotional elements of running a successful business. The term "success" encompasses both the financial and qualitative aspects of life. My aim is to clarify and reaffirm what is important to you, and uncover the emotional stumbling blocks that get in the way of your success. By the end of this chapter, you will be invited to consider the benefits of being accountable, and you will be given the tools to create a powerful pathway to fulfilling your dream lifestyle.

Along with the above, this chapter will highlight the relationship between changes in the dynamic of relationships, your emotional awareness, and your personal and business success. Emotional pressure, and the relationships that you have with others, play a key role – and this is one that we will examine in depth.

The advantages of being a solopreneur, or a small or medium-sized enterprise (SME) owner, include flexibility and choice. These two possibilities, together with ownership and responsibility, constitute the foundation of a successful business. Your interest in reading this chapter may well be because of your desire to create a successful business, and your passion for fulfilling a need in the marketplace. By reading this chapter, you will find the commitment to see this through – developing the necessary skills and acquiring the tools needed for long-term success. Finally, I will also teach you about the importance of developing resilience, so that you can deal with the inevitable challenges and setbacks that occur when building a business.

Instead of following fixed strategies, my suggestion is for you to develop an approach that is malleable, suits your purposes, and provides the answers to your own questions. By doing so, you will gain an understanding of what is needed to create and grow your business. You will also become aware of what is going on in the background – which, at first, may not seem obvious. Using my tips, you can develop the ability to identify and overcome the emotional blocks that may get in the way of a successful life.

Success is a very personal experience, so you must identify the elements that are an expression of what matters to you. By starting your own business, you put yourself on the line; you increase the level of risk and take responsibility for your life. What makes a difference, and provides clarity, is the development of ground rules and your own strategies that keep you on track. By investing time in considering all the aspects, including the emotional implications of having your own business, you will be able to monitor your progress and avoid surprises. The return on your time and money investment can be measured by the speed with which you resolve and deal with issues that will inevitably come up. This can also be measured by how fast you implement new business development initiatives. By the end of this chapter, you will be in a position to ensure that you gain and keep your clients, by providing a first class service – a service that reflects what success means to you.

There are two distinctive parts to this chapter, part one where I cover the "You" element of the business, and part two where I briefly cover other elements.

So, without further ado, let's begin!

You

For me, the following was a life-changing statement, because it made me reflect on my business approach:

"Some of you are flying in the business, some of you are struggling and some of you are in the middle. So, let's look at it, the products are the same, the business plan is the same. So, what differs is you. You are the variable. Make sure you work on yourself harder than on your business." – Jim Rohn, Business Philosopher.

The "You" is the variable element of the business. This element is complex and unique. It is impacted by your overall view of life, the emotional characteristics expressed depending on the role you play – whether that's the role of a business person, family member, or friend. The management of life as a solopreneur requires a different set of skills from those of an employee, and the expectations of all the various roles create different dynamics in how you live. This is more so at the initial stage of the business, when a small budget may limit the availability of resources.

We may be inspired by what is possible, and can see different opportunities when reading quotes such as:

- *"Whatever you can do or dream you can, begin it. Boldness has genius, power and magic in it!"* – Goethe
- *"I think it is possible for ordinary people to choose to be extraordinary."* – Elon Musk
- *"Be the change you want to see in the world."* – Mahatma Gandhi
- *"To have a great life is your birthright, vulnerability is part of your greatness, suffering is optional."* – Anna M Stapleton

Enthusiasm and a positive attitude are contagious, and are noticeable when they are present in our daily interactions. Liking and loving what you do are key factors to living a fulfilling life, which, of course, includes having a thriving business that you are proud of. But, how do you access enthusiasm, authentic motivation, and passion, when they are not naturally present? These characteristics are part of what one of my dear friends keeps reminding me: 'It is an inside job; no one can do it for you.'

It is up to each one of us to learn what motivates and excites us, and what the driving force is that makes us take action. We may start with enthusiasm but, over time, we become burdened with the reality of what it takes to start, build, and maintain a sustainable and profitable business. When that happens, most people simply give up. On paper, we can produce perfect strategies and plans, but the challenge is to ensure that they are followed and executed. A way to discover what is holding us back, is by understanding and embracing the complexity of the "You" part of running a business. Look at your mental attitude towards yourself, business, and life in general. Your mental attitude is impacted by many factors that enable you to succeed, and is also at the source of any emotional blocks preventing you from functioning at your full potential.

The characteristics of your mental attitude can be identified by answering these questions:

Q What do you really, really, really want?

Q What really matters to you?

Q Why are you doing what you are doing?

Q Why are you not doing what you said you would do?

By answering these questions, you will uncover what is important to you; you will also become aware of what stops you and what is in the way of your success. This is an opportunity to consider what is possible and what you are capable of. You can enquire and speculate on the different options available to you, and choose the one that resonates with your values and beliefs.

This process is very powerful. Its value and effectiveness are especially enhanced when done with others, be that with a coach, mentor, or mastermind group. Producing results is a pre-requisite for a successful business, but it can be very difficult to take an objective view of your performance. You therefore need authentic feedback, which will impact your thinking, level of clarity, and peace of mind. To have feedback from someone who observes your performance from the outside can be very encouraging, useful, and constructive. With this process, you can separate what is important and what makes the difference in what you want to achieve, from what gets in the way and does not move you forward. It is about appreciating the difference between what works and what does not work. What works are those elements that empower you and encourage you to take action. What does not work are those elements that prevent you from fulfilling your potential. For example, conversations that go round and round in your head, and lead nowhere. I call this mental clutter "the enemy within". By letting go of the mental clutter, it is possible to achieve peace of mind which feels real, is priceless, and leads to success.

When running a business, it is inevitable that there will be ups and downs. It's easy to deal with the ups, what matters is that you are strong enough to deal with the downs, and have what it takes to face the challenges powerfully. Any discrepancy between what you plan and the results you produce will highlight what you need to concentrate and focus on. The chances are, any discrepancy is due to either lack of expertise and know-how, or lack of awareness about the impact of emotional factors.

As we are looking at the "You" part of the business, the focus is on the possible factors that could impact your effectiveness, including those that could sabotage the creation of a solid foundation. These are the hidden emotional elements that may get in the way of a long-term successful business, and determine how you view life. The environment you grew up in, what you learnt through your parents, schooling, and social encounters, will all influence the way you approach your business, particularly when it comes to money, success, and failure.

Ownership and Responsibility

You are responsible for what happens in your life. Think about that statement for a moment. Say it out loud. You have ownership of your life, and your future. You make the decisions for your business, and in your personal life too. Ownership means taking control, and being responsible for your own change. It is very important to understand that ownership and responsibility are privileges. They are not burdens, and must be seen from the perspective of leadership. You are not waiting for circumstances to change around you, and you are not waiting for other people to change. You take responsibility for making your business work, and do whatever you need to do to achieve your goals.

Ownership and being responsible require developing the courage to recognise that whenever there is an issue, directly or indirectly, **you** have to do something about it. This does not mean that you are at fault or that you are to blame. Instead, it's about acknowledging that, in some way, you are involved, and thus will be involved in resolving the problem.

Personal Experience

Through the benefit of powerful coaching, it was pointed out to me that, when communicating, my tendency was to complain and make unhelpful comments about how things should or should not be. I was invited to consider that, whenever there was what I defined as a problem, I was there. I was also invited to think about what part I had played in arriving at the circumstances I found myself in. I did not like this process. In fact, at first, I felt threatened and quite uncomfortable. However, as I had asked for authentic and straight feedback, I was getting just what I needed. In that moment, I chose to see it as an opportunity for personal growth. I acknowledged that it was not about me personally, but rather the habits and behaviours I had developed as a result of my past conditioning. I experienced a "light bulb moment", which has changed the direction of my life. I recognised that I had a choice on how I related to what I was dealing with, including my relationship with ownership and responsibility. I did not invalidate myself, but simply recognised that I needed to expand my level of awareness about the world around me. I also acknowledged the importance of learning to deal with uncertainty, and trusting myself and others.

I am inviting you now to consider that the qualities of taking ownership and being responsible provide an opportunity. They give you the chance to choose how to react to circumstances, and to show that you are in charge of how things go in life. Have you ever found yourself in a position where, when dealing with a problem, more time is spent talking about whose fault it was or what someone did wrong, than finding a solution? Clearly, mistakes are made and things go wrong, but spending too much time analysing a problem does not move things forward.

Personal growth and development are what make you strong and capable of dealing with whatever comes your way; this is particularly relevant when you are faced with disempowering events, like a failed business venture. Occasions like this can lead to you drawing negative conclusions about your abilities as a businessperson. You cannot change the outcome of events, and you may have little control over external circumstances and phenomena. However, what is within your control is the way you relate to these circumstances, and what actions you take.

When you come from a position of ownership and responsibility, you can develop a powerful mental attitude. You can take the necessary actions to create a strong foundation for your business, and learn how to wipe the slate clean, take control, create a vision for yourself, and fulfil your purpose in life. The learning process that enables you to be successful includes:

- ✓ Managing past conditioning.
- ✓ Discovering the source of self-sabotage.
- ✓ Developing new habits.
- ✓ Understanding how you communicate.
- ✓ Learning how to fulfil your goals.

Managing Past Conditioning

How you react to circumstances is key to the quality of your life. Your reactions are determined by your expectations and beliefs, and by what makes you tick. To make the most from the understanding of past conditioning, it is paramount to appreciate the difference between being informed by the past and being limited by it.

Being informed by the past means that you learn from your experiences, and are aware of the choices you have made and their implications. Being limited by it means that you are not fully aware of what is going on at a subconscious level, and therefore not in control of your reactions and behavioural patterns.

Far too often, we are denied the enjoyment of a balanced life because of stress and frustration. On an emotional level, this is the result of not being aware of why we feel disempowered. You can regain your power by uncovering and dealing with what triggers you. This enables you to identify possible reasons for the loss of power, and to get to the source of why you aren't fulfilling your potential, or achieving the outcomes you want.

To have your life work the way you want it to work, it is important to discover whether your conscious and subconscious beliefs are congruent with each other. Beliefs, whether empowering or disempowering, consist of what you trust and accept as true. They are developed as you grow up and are shaped by your environment. They are also part of the inherited conditioning that you never question, unless you experience a situation which forces you to do so. Your subconscious mind, which acts as a filing cabinet, is totally non-judgmental. It accepts without question your beliefs, and stores them in the back of your mind. You may well get so busy with everything else that you are no longer conscious of these beliefs. However, they are still there, and their impact surfaces when you least expect it.

A very useful exercise is to make a list of the qualities that you believe your ideal business partner, parent, partner, sibling, and child should have. You could also make a list of the qualities you consider that you should possess, in the various roles you hold. Following this, compare these lists with the reality of both other people and yourself. The differences and discrepancies that show up in the comparisons will reveal possible sources of self-sabotage. They will also enable you to get to the source of your disappointments and upsets.

Exercise	
a.	List the qualities you expect from your ideal ....
b.	List the qualities you observe in the behaviour of ....
c.	Are there any discrepancies between a and b? If so, what impact do they have on the relationship?
d.	List the qualities you expect of yourself as a ....
e.	List the qualities you display of yourself as a ....
f.	Are there any discrepancies between d and e? If so, what impact do they have on the relationship you have with yourself?

The impact of the conditioning from past events is uncovered in different ways. One way is to find out the origin of discrepancies between expectations that come from past experiences and actual results. The result of this comparison highlights the discrepancy between the way you think or believe things should be, and how they actually are. This calls for authenticity in recognising what you really think, and acknowledging your beliefs, both on a conscious and subconscious level. The purpose of this process is to discover what is really going on, increase your level of awareness, and uncover hidden barriers. Now, answer the following questions:

Q What resentments or experiences of unfairness are you holding onto?

Q How can you become at peace with what happened with (particular person or circumstance)?

Q What undelivered communications do you have that need addressing with (specify who)?

Q How do you relate to money and wealth?

Q What is your definition of business success?

Q How do you relate to success and failure in business?

The answers to these questions will highlight issues that you may not be aware of, and you will be faced with the realisation that your choices have been clouded by the experience of past events – they are not based on the present reality. What matters is to consider the consequences of any unresolved conflicts or underlying beliefs, and their implications, on the nature and quality of your choices. The next section will provide further clarification.

Discovering the Source of Sabotage

We sabotage ourselves or our business because of some fundamental fear that we are not aware of. This is a fear that, consciously or subconsciously, we do not want to face. Sabotage is the result of the discrepancy between conscious and subconscious beliefs, and hidden agendas that result from past conditioning.

The way we deal with fear is also a source of sabotage, whether that's fear of failure or even fear of success, fear of being judged, fear of being rejected, or fear of being criticised. This leads to procrastination, or choices which are at odds with your business commitment. Uncovering the impact of these limiting fears makes a profound difference to your effectiveness and experience of personal power. Over the years, I have helped many clients to uncover what was going on in the background of their mind – things that they were not aware of.

Andrew B

I started working with Andrew 9 months after he left his job to start a HR consultancy business. He was clear about what he was offering, and what he wanted to do, but when it came to sending out proposals, he would procrastinate. After several conversations, it became clear that, although he had left his job, he was still holding a sense of resentment and disappointment towards his ex-boss. There was unfinished business that he had to deal with.

He recalled a very uncomfortable incident when he was still employed. He thought he had dealt with it, but clearly the impact of his upset was still at the back of his mind.

He recounted that during a reorganisational phase within the previous company he worked for, he was asked to write his own job description for his new role. He spent much time and effort in coming up with something he was excited about. He submitted the proposal and the new job description was approved. Within three months a conflict arose between Andrew and his boss. He would plan something based on the agreed role, and his boss would ask for something else.

Andrew felt quite confused. It got to the point when he said to his boss: 'I am just following what we agreed I should be doing.' The boss replied: 'I make the final decisions, and this is what you do.' This reply contradicted what had been agreed. Feeling extremely frustrated, Andrew decided to leave the company.

We considered the impact and implication of Andrew's emotional reaction to the circumstances of him leaving the company. He took ownership and responsibility for what had happened, and recognised that rather than communicating with his boss about the discrepancy between his job description and what his boss was asking him to do, he had stayed silent and complained about it to colleagues, friends, and family.

Part of Andrew's action plan was for him to get in touch with his ex-boss, to find out what really went on during this reorganisation. Initially, Andrew was quite reluctant, and could not see the point in this. We discussed the importance of not letting thwarted conversations linger. He decided to make an appointment with his ex-boss and went to see him. Beforehand, we mocked the conversation he was going to have with his ex-boss, Andrew was able to clarify his thought process which gave him the opportunity to practise communicating in a way that would not come across as resentful and upset.

The meeting happened. It had been very useful for Andrew to discover what was going on during the period prior to him leaving the company. He realised that the conclusions he had drawn about his boss's behaviour did not reflect accurately the facts. This conversation made a huge difference, so much so that his ex-boss was able to provide useful connections that led to Andrew obtaining his largest major client to date.

Loretta S

I worked with Loretta for 6 months. She was in her mid-20s, and worked as a Customer Service Manager within a medium size retail company. Although she was proud of her success and the way she was treated, she felt unfulfilled and wanted a change. She decided that she wanted to go into teaching.

Loretta completed the necessary research to narrow down where to go and what to do. However, I realised that something was not quite right when she missed a session, and was not keeping to her promises. We decided to look at what was going on in the background that perhaps she had not considered. Why was she sabotaging herself? As we went through a process of uncovering the possible blocks, she suddenly remembered that years earlier, when she was considering her career choices, she had investigated teaching. At some stage, she had created a belief that women only go into teaching so that they can combine work with family life, and Loretta had decided that this was something she would not do.

Years later, this belief contradicted her renewed interest in teaching! This was a great revelation to her, and the shift in her thinking and actions was remarkable. Within a short space of time she was able to secure a teaching job!

Martin C

As a chartered accountant, Martin wanted to develop his own training company. He had the necessary training and expertise, and had identified a gap in the market. His intention was to make use of freelance trainers and subcontractors. However hard he tried though, he seemed unable to find the right people to work with. He would get as far as drafting contracts, and then something would happen that meant the arrangements didn't go ahead.

Martin felt rather frustrated and despondent. We worked together over a period of a few months. He identified his main limiting belief to be: 'People can't be trusted. They only connect with you when they want something from you.' This went back to a series of incidents that happened when he was training as an accountant.

I asked Martin to consider in what other areas trust was missing, and the impact this was having on his business and personal life. Martin also agreed to be in communication with the people he was involved with during his training. Within a short period of time, Martin obtained a level of mental clarity that made a huge difference to the success of his company.

Brian S

Brian is a successful professional who deals with compliance. He is highly trained and effective. We have worked together for a number of years. One day I happened to be in his office, and I was rather surprised to see him behaving in a flustered and agitated manner. I asked whether he was ok to which he replied, 'This client drives me mad! Do I really need all this aggravation?' I asked him whether he would be prepared to work with me and get to the bottom of his frustration. He agreed.

I asked him to describe his relationship with this client, and what it was that he found difficult and frustrating. Brian replied, 'He is so demanding and pedantic, he reminds me of my father!' He then started laughing. He realised that this client was triggering emotions he felt when he was younger, dealing with his father. This had been going on for a long time, and there was a real danger that he would let the client go, just because the relationship was not as Brian wanted it to be. We did some more work on the whole issue, and he adopted a simple strategy that, whenever he had to contact this client, in addition to the technical element of the call, he would prepare himself mentally to ensure that he would not fall into the trap of being triggered.

Brian also acknowledged that, although his reaction to this client was quite extreme and strong, there was a common pattern in his reaction to other clients, and how he reacted to their demands. The practice of preparing himself emotionally before talking to this and other clients has paid off. Brian has been able to manage his reactions to their demands to such an extent that, to this day, he experiences an increased level of mental clarity and effectiveness. He no longer suffers from frustration and annoyance at the end of phone conversations. He has been using one of my strategies, StopByDesign, which includes acknowledging the current circumstances as well as the emotional implications of the situation in hand. Brian's awareness of the possible triggers and his willingness for these not to be reactivated, give him real control over his emotions. Over time, the intensity of his negative emotions has diminished.

These examples highlight the importance of not allowing decisions made in the past to cloud your judgement and actions for current circumstances. The usefulness of "letting go of the mental clutter" can be measured by the increased level of effectiveness in the task in hand.

In their book, *Tapping into Ultimate Success*, Jack Canfield and Pamela Bruner describe the importance of dealing with negative emotions to succeed both in business and in life. The book covers how Emotional Freedom Technique (EFT), also known as Tapping, is used to remove emotional blocks and achieve success. EFT is a powerful holistic healing technique that has been proven to effectively resolve emotional issues caused by past events. It can be used as a self-help method, and is based on the combined principles of ancient Chinese acupressure and modern psychology. By tapping with the fingertips on specific meridian endpoints of the body, while focusing on negative emotions or physical sensations, it is possible to calm the nervous system. This process helps the brain to respond in healthy and positive ways, and to restore the balance of energy in the body.

Developing New Habits

Our economic and social landscape is changing at an astonishing rate, and there is a real need to keep up with these changes and adjust to the reality of modern living. By getting rid of unnecessary mental clutter, you will have more mental space to develop new things, including new habits that in turn will support you in achieving what you want. So, the quality of your life, both in general and in business, is manifested by the type and quality of your habits – which show up in your behaviour.

It is therefore important to assess whether the habits you hold are up-to-date and congruent with what is going on around you. If not, they need to be changed and adjusted to the new reality. Otherwise, you run the risk of keeping habits just because they are familiar and make you feel comfortable – without becoming aware of the cost of holding onto them. The cost can be measured in terms of time, money, or quality of life. Furthermore, keeping habits that no longer serve you is another form of sabotage, because they get in the way of fulfilling new and different goals.

In order for any type of change to happen, and last over time, a conscious effort must to be made to deal with what needs changing. You must also be willing to let go of the inherent resistance to change that is normally experienced by human beings. A new habit can only be made permanent via consistent practise, and by creating a structure that reinforces it; this is a process that can be learnt.

It is important to consider the change of habits required when transitioning from employee to solopreneur. Those habits which were useful when employed, may become a hindrance when faced with the requirements of running a business.

Personal Example

Over a period of 25 years, I have been involved with various businesses. This is the experience I had when I started an additional business with a very limited budget. The habits I had developed, and used to produce results in the corporate environment, became a hindrance as a solopreneur.

For example, as a team leader in the corporate world, I was effective at delegating and developing the members of my team. I was used to making requests and, without much effort, I got what I needed. As a solopreneur, however, I had no team to delegate to and no specialist reference point. I soon realised that I did not have the inclination, patience, and skills to complete some of the basic things that needed to be done. My attention got diverted from building a client base to trying to manage and complete the administrative and logistical tasks. I would agonise over questions like 'What is the most effective use of my time?' or 'What should I do first?' I would waste entire mornings without accomplishing much. I had not foreseen the impact my work habits as an employee would have on my effectiveness as a solopreneur, and the need to adjust to the new circumstances.

Although it is still work in progress, what has enabled me to make a shift has been the willingness to go back to basics and take each task in turn (i.e. inputting information on the database), the patience to learn new tasks (i.e. learning how to set up of a power point presentation), gaining clarity on the type of resources available (paid and free), and making a choice on how to use them. This has been possible mainly because of the development of new habits.

Understanding How You Communicate

Communication is an extremely important topic, and has a strong bearing on the way we connect with our surroundings and express the way we see the world. The words we use reflect the world we live in, what is important to us, and how we relate to it. They describe our philosophy of life and articulate our commitment to ourselves and our business. Communication is not limited to what we communicate externally, but also to what we say to ourselves. In fact, what we say to ourselves has more of an impact on our success than what we say externally.

There is an emotional common thread between past conditioning, the words we use when communicating, the development of new habits, and the fulfilment of goals. This common thread is determined by the subtle, pervasive messages that reflect our core beliefs, and those that we subconsciously repeat to ourselves day in and day out. By uncovering this, we can gain clarity and guidance on how to carry out our daily activities, and understand how we are perceived. The words and tone we use to describe ourselves and our business reflect how we view the world, because they express what is going on for us.

I have covered the importance of managing past conditioning, the dangers of sabotage, the existence of supportive habits, and the impact of how we communicate. I am now going to consider the future, and how to manifest what you want to achieve.

Learning How to Fulfil Your Goals

The fulfilment of goals is a combination of knowing what you want to achieve, maintaining your commitment over time, taking appropriate action, and producing the desired results. This can be achieved by creating a supportive structure around you, which consists of specific processes, knowledge, and experts you can rely on. I now want to cover the impact that affirmations can have on what you want to achieve, and fulfil your goals.

Affirmations are statements that express your positive intentions and desired goals. They are not set in stone, and their effectiveness is measured by how they make you feel when you verbalise them. When they no longer inspire and motivate you, then they have become obsolete. Their value is experienced when used as fear breakers and belief creators. When used properly, affirmations enable you to voice your deepest desires and goals, and help you to get to the heart of what it would take to accomplish your goals. They can be used as a reference point, like a compass.

Personal Example

As part of my training and development, many years ago, I created what has become my constant affirmation. This acts as my compass:

'What matters to me is the practice of leadership, commitment and love.'

Whenever in doubt, I remind myself of what is important to me and why I do it. I then go through a process that enables me to regain equilibrium, and from that space I decide on a fresh plan of action.

Together with the development of new habits, affirmations will help you to reboot your past conditioning, and pull things together to keep a positive energy flowing. They also help you to enhance the general level of your wellbeing by reducing the immediate "fight, flight, or freeze" response. By slowing down and taking time to reflect, you will make better decisions and take appropriate actions.

For affirmations to be effective, they need to be short enough that you can memorise and remember them easily. They must include words that convey excitement, correspond to strong emotional experiences – such as joy – and express what you want to achieve. They also need to be written in the first person, and articulated at a time when you feel happy, satisfied, and uplifted – reflecting the emotions that you would feel as a result of achieving your goals.

The creation of affirmations is part of my StopByDesign coaching approach. As part of the process, the client verbalises one or more affirmations which put him/her in a positive, powerful state of mind. I then invite the client to rate themselves on a scale of 1-10 daily, and communicate the rating to me. At the next session, we look at what circumstances have impacted the rating, and find out whether there are any triggers or repetitive patterns that require further attention. Finally, I guide the client to recreate the affirmation to get back to a powerful state of mind. From that space, we create the next action plan.

Anthony Y

Anthony is a very successful solopreneur in the building industry. He is a millionaire. The joy, fulfilment, and benefits of his business success are negatively impacted by family circumstances that he wants to change. He has hired me to coach him on how to deal with personal issues that clearly are not working for him. As part of the process, he has created an affirmation that gives him power: 'I feel free, loving and authentic with my family.'

Anthony has identified specific actions that will make a difference in achieving this goal and move things forward with his family. We are still working together.

This is an example of the importance of ensuring that the "You" element is operating effectively, to enjoy the benefits of having a healthy bottom line in business. It is interesting to note that, despite Anthony's wealth, his affirmation includes the desire to feel free.

Your Business

Having covered the "You" part of your business, what follows is a short synopsis of the other elements needed to build a solid business. These elements have also been covered in greater details in other chapters of the book:

- ✓ Articulate your message.
- ✓ Find your contacts.

- ✓ Build a client base.
- ✓ Create a brand and differentiate yourself.
- ✓ Share content.
- ✓ Maintain growth.
- ✓ Follow up.

Articulate Your Message

The awareness of what motivates you and the nature of your chosen business, will enable you to develop and verbalise your message. This message needs to be delivered in a style that meets the expectations of your marketplace. Furthermore, it must reflect the vision and mission of your business. You articulate your message by developing a pitch which describes the product or service you offer, and the type of problem it solves for the client. The pitch also must include what you are looking for and a call-to-action statement.

Find Your Contacts

Although there are many methods to finding contacts, the one I want to emphasise is face-to-face networking. This type of networking can be very enjoyable, but also time consuming. The choice of networking groups and level of participation requires careful consideration, and needs to make business sense. Business networking cannot be confused with the desire to fulfil other emotional needs.

Personal Example

At a personal level, another of my main challenges has been balancing the need for social contact against the development of the business. When I was in the corporate world, my social needs were easily met by mixing with work colleagues. However, after I left, I struggled with the experience of isolation and the desire to be with other people. I joined many networking groups, where the people were very nice and supportive, however my focus was not so much on building the business, but on satisfying the need of belonging. I have now become more selective on the frequency and type of networking events I go to, and I keep under review the effectiveness of my choices.

While this could be considered an oversimplification, because the social element can be an integral part of developing a business, it is important to have a strategic approach to the choice of how and where to connect with the right audiences for your business, and monitor the quality of contacts.

Build a Client Base

The identification of who you want to work with is at the core of ensuring you match your offerings to your clients' objectives and needs. The clarity of your answers to the following questions will support you in matching what you offer with your clients' needs and requirements:

- **Q** What skills and experience do I have, which help me to solve my clients' problems?
- **Q** How can I add value to my clients' requests?
- **Q** What other requirements might my clients have in the future, that they are not yet aware of?
- **Q** What relevant success stories can I share with my clients, so that they can gain a deeper understanding of what I can offer them?

The building of a client base requires time, patience, persistence, and the ability to deal with objections. I invite you to consider that your prospects are divided into various categories:

(a) 'Yes'

(b) 'No'

(c) 'I am interested, but …'

(d) 'No, because ...'

The 'Yes' answers are easy to manage, and they quickly become part of the next phase of the business process. The 'No' answers are clear cut – if there is no matching of offerings to the needs. However, 'No' may not be a definite response, and may well be influenced by timing and needs, which can change over time. In this case, it pays to have clarity on whether the 'No' is forever, or leaves an open door for the future. The ones I find most interesting, and provide further attention to, are the prospects who say, 'I am interested but …' or 'Not now but …' without giving a straight answer. The 'No because' also requires further investigation, because by identifying the reasons for rejection, you can determine the nature of the objection.

The learnings from the first part of the chapter could be applied in this context, to gain a better understanding of where the customer is coming from. This could make a real difference in finding out the real reason behind their answers.

Personal Example

I have had very interesting conversations with prospects who could not decide whether they wanted to work with me. If I consider it to be appropriate, I will challenge them, and ask why they won't give me a straight answer. I listen, make no comments, and just acknowledge their concerns. This process enables them to overcome their hesitation, and come to a decision. Even though the conversation may not result in a sale, at least I know where I stand.

Apart from the clear 'No' answers, all the other categories must be included in the appropriate section of the follow up process.

Create Your Brand and Differentiate Yourself

Attracting the *right* client is a function of creating a personal branding and differentiation. The internet – which provides easy access to information and the alternatives available to potential clients – is a big challenge that you face, and must overcome, in order to be heard and be noticed. What makes the difference is how what you offer distinguishes you from what others offer, and how they present themselves.

The element that is unique is **your** story. Your story builds a connection with the people who can relate to it; it communicates your message and reveals your uniqueness. The development of your story enables you to promote the value of what you offer, reaffirms what matters to you, and establishes what you want to be remembered for. Those who relate to you and what you offer will become your clients.

Share Content

There are many ways to increase your level of visibility and credibility, whether that be through presentations, blogs, videos, books and articles, or other written material. Sharing what you know, creates content and connects you with your audience. It gives you the opportunity to educate your clients and prospects, and at the same time become recognised as an expert or thought leader in your field.

For a physical product, the content that you can share could consist of tips and advice on its characteristics and how to use it. This information can prove to be very useful, and will add value to the purchase of the product. As a mentor, coach, consultant, speaker, or trainer, you can inform and educate your audience by sharing useful information based on your training and your own life experiences. This can enhance and support others in their own growth and development.

Maintain Growth

Every business goes through at least two stages of development. The first is the formulation, and the other is the momentum stage. It is important to be aware of the stage you are at, because they will each require different actions. At the formulation/ initial stage, it will be necessary to put a lot of effort into developing the steps that I have described so far, for limited returns. However, as momentum builds and you learn and practise the various activities of the business, the ratio between time spent on the business and your levels of return will change. This may require an analysis on how and where you spend your time. For example, you may reallocate time from generating new leads to following up with existing contacts. What matters most is appreciating the stage you are at, and taking the appropriate action. This knowledge will provide useful information when preparing your marketing plan, and deciding on the timing of the various activities you may become involved with. It can also be useful when dealing with the emotional impact of analysing your results. It is well documented that during the initial stage of any business, it is necessary to put a lot of effort in, just for limited returns. It is therefore important not to become demotivated or invalidate yourself if the results are not as you may have wanted. Growth maintenance depends on a consistent level of engagement and a strong marketing strategy.

Follow Up

Another quote from Business Philosopher Jim Rohn, that I believe is very relevant and important to your business is, "The fortune is in the follow up." The success of your business rests on the continuity and quality of contact with your existing clients and your visibility within your chosen niche. This is achieved through sharing content and the implementation of an appropriate marketing strategy. By doing this, you will attract the right people, who will become your clients and who will come back to you – because they know, trust, and become loyal to you.

Key Learnings:

The following key learnings are part of a continuous process of business development and need to be analysed and updated regularly. They must not be treated as "one offs":

- ✓ Consider your emotional state and make a note of any possible negative implications to the success of your business.
- ✓ Consider the different roles you have and how they interrelate with each other. Is there any emotional fallout you need to think about?

- ✓ Consider the emotional implications of your decisions and the impact they have on the business.
- ✓ Make a list of the expectations you have of yourself, in the various roles you hold. Compare them with the reality of how you operate in these roles. Any discrepancy will give you clues about the areas you need to work on.
- ✓ Whenever you start a business with someone you already know, consider what you know about each other, and what could interfere with the business relationship.
- ✓ Be mindful of the fact that you already have an existing relationship with the person. Depending on the circumstances, there may already be hidden expectations, opinions, and assumptions on how things will develop in the business relationship.
- ✓ A change in the type of relationship will bring a change in dynamics, and you need to ensure the impact is a positive one.
- ✓ Whenever there is a change of circumstances, ensure you deal with any "unfinished business". Unresolved issues that have not been acknowledged or dealt with properly, become emotional baggage.
- ✓ Any outstanding issue could hinder and slow your business growth. This can lead to self-sabotage or sabotage of the business.
- ✓ Gaining a clearer and better understanding of the circumstances will change the way you relate to the same situation. You can then recreate the relationship, based on the new information.
- ✓ Research and learn techniques, for example Emotional Freedom Technique (EFT) or Tapping, that could enable you to reduce and eliminate the emotional charge caused by everyday activities.
- ✓ Develop strategies that give you a structure of how to organise your thoughts and plan your actions.
- ✓ Ensure you are clear on the vision and the service you provide.
- ✓ Maintain credibility by being involved with organisations and institutions which would recognise you as an expert.
- ✓ Follow up with your clients and contacts.
- ✓ Work with a coach who can support you in clarifying your thinking and hold you to account.

Summary

One of the biggest advantages of being a solopreneur and having your own business is to have flexibility on how you operate. In this chapter, the emphasis has been on the possible and hidden emotional aspects of the "You", and how they impact the way a business is created and developed. These elements should be included in the feasibility study of the business. Once you have matched the "You" part of the business with what you offer, you are ready to articulate a compelling message that resonates with your ideal clients. You will be able to gain clients and keep them, by meeting their requirements and satisfying their needs. This can be achieved through the implementation of strategies and approaches which lead to the profitability and success of the business.

Both the emotional elements of running a business and the implementation of strategies and processes to ensure success of the business, need to be managed over time. This can be achieved by ensuring the availability of adequate support, to ensure the maintenance of objectivity, positivity, and consistency of action. Coaches, mentors, mastermind groups, or accountability partners are powerful resources who can support you in ensuring you keep to your promises and fulfil your goals. They are on your side, and are committed to your success.

You have the right to succeed. The resources are available to you – so go for it! You deserve it!

Biography

Anna M Stapleton is a qualified Life Coach with Noble Manhattan Coaching, Ltd and an Emotional Freedom Technique (EFT) Practitioner. Her professional background and experience enable her to offer coaching and mentoring services internationally. Her experience within the HR corporate environment, the Personal Growth, Training and Development Industry and the Mental Health Sector of the NHS motivates her to promote Mental and Emotional Wellbeing.

In her chapter, Anna highlights the importance of distinguishing between the logistical and the emotional elements of running a business and learning how to manage them powerfully. The increased level of awareness improves effectiveness and contributes to living a balanced life.

https://www.readytomakeachange.com/

Anna is also an Accredited Master Coach (AMC) for the IAPC&M and is listed in the online directory https://coach-accreditation.services/directories/find-an-accredited-coach-or-mentor/.

CHAPTER FIVE

By

Maria Hocking

Heart-Led Marketing

Winning clients is not about waiting for clients. I discovered this many years ago, sat in my newly decorated office. Staring at the telephone, willing it to ring, I prayed for a call. After 3 hours, half a pack of chocolate digestives, and far too much coffee, I concluded that randomly giving out a few business cards wasn't going to bring clients through the door.

Taking a step back to reflect, I changed my strategy. Applying learnings gained not only from my previous businesses, but from life itself, I began to see results. My once empty diary began to fill with daily client appointments. I went from having zero clients, to a few clients, and then on to having many clients. The next stage was recognising that I had **too** many clients! This resulted in me making necessary changes within the business, to lower the quantity and increase client quality. Having put the work in at the beginning to win and keep clients, my business now runs very successfully, primarily through recommendation.

You too can experience the same success, and you do not have to figure it out alone. Winning clients is not about luck, and it's not about having the most beautiful website. It's not dependent on heavy financial marketing investment, having the most expensive business suit, or having the best business card. Winning and keeping clients is about people. Simple as. Never, ever forget that. Winning hearts and creating powerful, authentic relationships, connecting with people and building valued relationships – all these things will contribute enormously to your success. I'm not talking about winning hearts during office hours, or from 9 to 5, but **always**. It doesn't require you to work 24/7; it simply means that you do it so much that it becomes part of who you are.

"The master in the art of living makes little distinction between his work and his play, his labour and his leisure, his mind and his body, education and religion. He hardly knows which is which; he simply pursues his vision of excellence in whatever he does, leaving others to decide whether he is working or playing. To him he is always doing both." – James Michener

With practise, creating opportunities to "light up lives" and make a difference wherever you go becomes the norm. Connecting with hearts becomes something that you very much enjoy. Give expecting nothing, and you will find yourself with everything. This includes many, many clients.

I didn't learn the above from a book, or a mentor, but through life itself. Years ago, I experienced a sustained period of adversity – a period in my life when, due to external circumstances, I lost me. My confidence and what felt like my identity disappeared within a very short time. Not believing that I was "enough", I just wanted to shrink away and disappear. One day, a stranger took the time to gently hold my arm, look me right in the eyes, and offer me some kind words. She lifted my day, and my life, and I will never forget how she made me feel. Shortly after that, I discovered this famous quote:

"Imagine everyone that you meet has a sign on their head that says, Make Me Feel Important. Not only will you succeed in sales, but succeed in life." – Mary Kay Ash

Recall a time when someone made you feel valued and important. Think about a customer or client experience that you had, that you still remember to this day. Recall a moment in time, when just **one person** made you feel so special, that they totally won your heart. It's very likely that you have either used their services again, or highly recommended them to others. To ensure that your business succeeds, you need to be the person that they come back to, and highly recommend.

If you're winning hearts, people will remember you, and remember your impact. Creating an impact and adding value to lives wherever you go will create strong foundations for your success. Personally recognising the benefits of this very early on in my career, led to the creation of my P.A.V.E Solopreneur Success Model. This model forms a solid structure for heart-led marketing and will be discussed in detail throughout this chapter.

It's important to understand that "heart wins" will result not only in direct clients, but referrals from the hearts of those clients. Many books suggest asking for referrals to win clients, which can be an effective strategy. I, however, have **never**, **ever** asked for a referral. I've never asked for one, because I've not needed to. They ask for me. When you start winning clients, through unrequested referrals, your business will flourish.

The Power of One Heart

With practise, winning hearts becomes easy and highly rewarding in so, so many ways. It's easier than you think, because your focus should be on quality not quantity! Understanding the power of "one" is paramount because:

- You are better off focusing on having a deep conversation with one person, than having surface conversations with many. Connecting with one heart is more effective than being in many heads. Having one person ask for your business card, is better than you wildly dishing them out to all.
- One client is not just a client for 6 weeks, 3 months, or 1 year. Your 1 client can be your client for life. When you truly appreciate and value your clients, they will return time and time again.

- One treasured client can lead to many, many clients and opportunities. (From single clients, I have gained not only multiple single clients, but much bigger clients such as schools, businesses and organisations.)

Never underestimate the power of one person with one heart. Starting out in business, we often prioritise quantity over quality. Reverse it. Aim for quality conversations with fewer people. Aim for powerful conversations, deep connections, and cosy "heart-warmth".

THE P.A.V.E Model - Four Key Components

I believe that heart-led marketing is the most efficient and effective way to not only win clients, but to keep them. Within heart-led marketing, I have personally identified four key areas that are essential for success; together they form the P.A.V.E solopreneur success model:

P – Passionate

A – Attentive

V – Vocal

E – Exceptional

To express the importance of these components, imagine for one moment, that you need a service or product. You have a choice of two paths, which both lead to your requirements. One path is full of pot holes, and the edges are not clearly defined. It's not obvious where the path goes or ends. Walking this path, you are not sure if you will ever find what you need. How committed would you be to walk this way?

The other path, however, consists of evenly laid bricks, and is very clearly defined. It is smooth, and its direction is obvious. It appears that taking the clearly defined route will allow you to find and access your required service or product, confidently and with ease. How likely would you be to walk **this** way?

As solopreneurs, we need to show our clients the way. We need to create the path of least resistance, so that they can follow and gain the results that they desire and need. We need to **pave the way** to success, for us both.

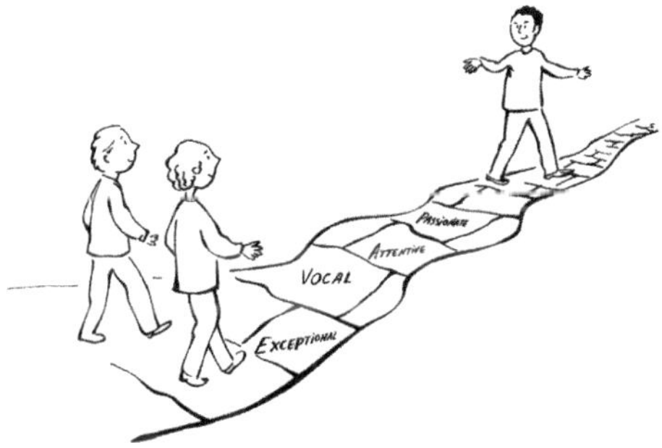

Think of the 4 elements of the solopreneur success model as bricks, laid repeatedly along the path that you create for your clients. We must ensure that we "lay all 4 of these bricks repeatedly" to pave the way for our clients. If we neglect to pay attention to one or more of the above components, and "miss out bricks", then our clients will stumble on their way to us. They may choose to look elsewhere and follow an easier path to find their solution.

Over the next few pages, we will explore each of these components individually. Having interviewed and spoken with many highly successful coaches, practitioners, and therapists over the years, I am aware that they exude extreme confidence and excel in all these areas. They lay their paths as true professionals. Thus, people not only follow, but actively seek these people and their services. Ensuring that you pay attention to and excel in these areas will result in you experiencing the same success.

PASSIONATE: attentive. vocal. exceptional

What Will I Learn?

- You have all that you need.
- The importance of identifying your beliefs.

The definition of "passion" in the Oxford Dictionary warmed my heart. "Strong and barely controllable emotion", very aptly summarises my own personal interpretation of this word. Compare it to having champagne in your veins; it's the "fizz" that you feel. Passion has been the driving force of my business from day one, and continues to be to this day. Your "barely controllable emotion" or "excitement" will push you through fear of not knowing enough or not being enough. It will drive you to constantly grow and learn, so that you can deliver an outstanding service. It will not allow you to wallow in perceived failure, but will drive you forwards to deliver better results, again and again and again.

- **Passion creates excitement. Passion attracts clients.**
- **Passion combined with belief, wins clients.**

If you have a passion for your service, **then you have all that you need.** Please re-read that last sentence. Pack those words into your heart, and know that you are enough. The small things that initially seem like the really big things, such as website design, social media, or keeping accounts, are all skills that can be easily learnt or outsourced. Passion CANNOT be taught or acquired. No-one can tip the champagne into your veins for you. It's either there, or it's not. Simple as! If you don't feel passion for your product or service, then walk away and find something that does make you feel "barely uncontrollable emotion".

Passion will also enable you to walk your talk, and you need to do this. You need to be seriously congruent in all that you say and do. The way that you live must reflect the message you want to deliver. Be your brand and be totally committed to your brand.

Why Passion Wins Clients

To win clients, you need to make them feel excited about the possibility of working with you. They need to feel or believe that you can solve their problem. They need to know that you are their solution. Your words alone are not enough. When you are passionate about what you do and offer, your words to others will be strong and authentic. This goes way beyond just words. It goes deep into the abyss of unconscious communication!

To understand this, recall a time when you saw somebody fall or hurt themselves. Did you feel yourself flinch? Or, how about this – have you ever spent time around negative people, and came away feeling drained? These feelings were likely created by the Mirror Neuron System (MNS) in your brain. The MNS was discovered by researchers Gallese and Rizzolatti at the University of Parma in Italy. They found that we have specific brain cells (mirror neurons) that fire both when we act, and when we observe the same action that is performed by another. If you watch someone playing football, your brain cells will fire as if YOU are playing football. If you closely watch someone eat a chocolate cake, then your brain will light up, as if YOU are eating the chocolate cake. Mirror neurons activate personal reactions within us, which reflect the actions or intentions of another.

So, you might be asking, how does eating chocolate cake apply to winning clients?

If we are passionate, then we will communicate this. Our own personal micro-expressions will be recognised by the MNS of a potential client. They will experience a little bit of what we feel. By showing your passion, it's likely that they will literally be "feeling" your passion. Emotion is contagious. It's likely that your clients will feel lifted through talking to you. They will then want more. Through passion, you can not only tell people that you can help them, but make them FEEL as if you can help them. You, just by being YOU, can make people excited about the possibility of experiencing your services.

It should be mentioned that yes, it is important to see the world through "the eyes of our clients", to help us understand their needs. We need to bear in mind that building rapport with a potential client is a big priority. If a client feels "stuck in the mud" then we need to dive into the mud with them. We need to see what they see, hear what they hear, and feel what they feel. We need to fully understand their problem. But we also need to show them that we have the solution. Your passion will help you to convey this.

Finding and Defining Your Power Within Passion

The next step is to clearly identify WHY you feel passionate about your service. Identifying the beliefs attached to your passion is essential. Identifying beliefs will not only motivate you, but enable you to become really clear about who your target market is, and where to find them.

You may have beliefs such as:

- The world needs to know about my service.
- It is my life purpose to deliver my skills and knowledge to help others.
- I believe that I can change lives.

Identifying your own beliefs about your skills and expertise will then allow you to really understand **who** and **where** your potential clients are. This can be done by taking each belief individually and drilling down to extract more information.

Example:

Q Who specifically in the world needs to know about this?

Q Who specifically would benefit from my skills and knowledge?

Q Whose lives could I change?

Then ask yourself:

Q Where could I find these people?

Q What could I do to connect with the people that would benefit from my help?

Q How can I win the hearts of potential clients?

Identifying these beliefs will also help you to understand and overcome the fear of many solopreneurs: **selling**. Ditch the concept of selling. I dare you to write the word "selling" on a piece of paper, right now. Then rip the paper and the word into a thousand tiny pieces! And write this down instead: *I am not selling. I am serving.*

This is not about you, but about your clients. Do not deny them what they need. Don't let them stay with a problem. Share with them your solution.

Passion + Identified Beliefs = Unstoppable Success!

Key Learnings:

- ✓ When I have passion, I have all that I need.
- ✓ Identifying the beliefs behind my passion is essential.
- ✓ I am not selling, I am serving.

passionate. ATTENTIVE. vocal. exceptional.

What Will I Learn?

- Why attentiveness is essential to winning clients.
- How to be more attentive.

How attentive are you? How closely do you listen and observe? If you were to rate your own attentiveness in general, on a scale of 1 to 10 (10 being highly attentive), what number would you be?

You need to aim for a 10 – nothing less. At a 10, you will maximise your chances of not only winning, but keeping clients.

Every single day, you will encounter many, many people. Some may simply pass you in the street; others may serve you in a shop or deliver you a parcel. You are surrounded by hundreds of potential opportunities to create clients. My question to you, is are you seeing them? Being attentive is about paying attention to others, and being concerned about their needs. It's about noticing the tiny details that most people choose to ignore. It's about spotting problems and offering solutions. The problem may simply be that an elderly person struggles with their shopping bags, and the solution is that you offer to help. Or it may be that you start a conversation with a stranger on a train, and discover that your services could be of great benefit. I'd now like to share with you one of my own personal experiences, which demonstrates the sheer power of attentiveness.

Personal Experience

A few years ago, my family and I went to a restaurant that we'd visited on many occasions. We had grown to love the restaurant, but over time had noticed that small things had started to slip. This made our experience there less and less pleasurable. The menu had changed significantly, the staff seemed unhappy, and nothing seemed particularly clean.

Overhearing other customers commenting on dropping standards, I decided to try and help. Later that day, I emailed the manager with constructive feedback. Re-assuring him that I wasn't complaining, I informed him of my observations. I said that if it was my restaurant, then I'd want to know what people were saying so that I could make improvements. Just thirty minutes later, I received a response:

"Thank you, Maria, for your feedback. It was very much appreciated. We have been through a very challenging time here within the business and have lost a couple of key members of staff. I had no idea that our cleanliness standards had dropped too and will take that into account and act on every observation. As for our staff, we treasure them greatly and want to support them fully. I see from your email signature that you are a motivational trainer. Would you be interested in coming in for a chat about delivering training for our staff?"

Four weeks later, I delivered multiple training programmes for the whole restaurant team. By being attentive to the needs of others, I'd created an opportunity. And it got even better than that. A year later, one of the staff members was working elsewhere. Guess who they recommended for staff training? Not to mention the three individual coaching clients that I gained as a result!

After accidentally discovering this strategy, I've continued to use it, and recommend that you use it too. Be more attentive. If you can see improvements that can be made, or needs that can be met, then contact appropriate people. (Ensure you have a business email signature, too.) Some may reply and thank you, but won't require your services. Others will be happy to speak further, and may hire you. As for those that don't reply? It doesn't matter. Just know that you have sown a seed that could turn into a tree-bearing fruit, in the form of clients. And if it doesn't? Simply hold your head high, knowing that you did a little something to make the world a better place.

My recommendation is that you practise being more attentive, aiming to become an observational expert! Following the tips below will enable you to develop skills in this area, and create clients as a result.

See Everyone as an Equal

Underneath business suits, dreadlocks, and job titles, we are all human beings. By seeing everyone as equal, you will have better and more open conversations, and be more confident in approaching people. Ensure that you talk with people, rather than at them.

Be Curious

Develop a desire to know more about people you meet. Start conversations anywhere and everywhere. Make it your mission to start at least one new conversation every day with someone that you have barely or never spoken with. Find out as much as you can about the people that you meet. For example:

- **Q** How long has your taxi driver been driving a taxi? What did he or she do previously?
- **Q** Is the gentleman sat next to you on a plane flying for business, or pleasure?
- **Q** How long has your barista been serving coffees? How much do they enjoy their job?
- **Q** Why does that frail elderly lady sit on the park bench alone, at the same time every day?

Understand that everyone has a story to tell. Give them the opportunity to share their experiences. This could not only change your business, but your life. Never underestimate the power of curiosity.

Look at Faces Not Phones

Whilst at networking conferences, meetings, or events, turn off your phone. I'd recommend leaving it in the car, so you are not tempted. It's all too easy to bury our faces into our phones when in a room full of strangers, so that we don't look or feel alone. Instead, look around for others that seem a little lost, and strike up a conversation. Connect with a heart. The more you practise doing this, the more your confidence will grow. If you feel anxious, then recognise that your anxiety is often created by worrying about what others will think of you. Flip this thought. It's not about you. It's about them. You are helping someone who looks alone, feel not quite so alone. Another top tip is to tell yourself that you are giving them the pleasure of your company for a few minutes (obviously don't say this out loud, just think it!). You will find yourself standing taller and feeling more confident, and able to start a conversation.

Understand that winning clients is not about luck. It's about the opportunities that you create, at every given opportunity. In a room full of strangers, there are many potential clients. Make it your mission to win hearts and clients whenever you can.

Practice ACTIVE listening

Summarised, active listening will communicate to the speaker: 'Yes, I hear and understand you'. It involves being fully present in that moment, and listening attentively. As a result, you will receive more information from the speaker, and really understand that information. To win and keep clients, it is essential that you fully comprehend their situation, and build trust and rapport. Being an active listener will help you to do this. To practice active listening:

- Stay focused whilst listening. Imagine a bubble around you both, and ignore other conversations.
- Never judge.
- Keep an open mind.
- Paraphrase and repeat the speaker's words back to them. (This will also help you understand their emotions.)
- Nod, smile, or say 'yes' occasionally, to show that you are listening.
- Put your own thoughts on hold; do not allow yourself to think about what you want to say next, whilst they are still talking.
- Do not interrupt.
- Make eye contact.

A good example of all the above, was a chiropractor I met. Years ago, suffering from a bad back, I rang to make an appointment with him, and discovered that he had a waiting list that was months long. Speaking about this with friends, it became clear that there was something very special about this man. Although he was clearly very skilled, it appeared that his success was not just down to his skills, but to his ability to connect with people. One of his clients shared these words:

"It's his connection with people. He is not an ordinary chiropractor. He can read you and your feelings very accurately. Lovely man, always smiling and happy. He is also very open about himself and his life. Practically my whole family see him. My friend's mum says he is a saviour. It's worth the wait to become his patient."

Understand now, that your ability to be truly attentive will play a huge part in your success as a solopreneur. Not only will you win more clients, but you will keep them – potentially forever. Your skills are important, but not as important as the way that you notice people and make them feel. Developing your attentiveness can be compared to removing your "blinkers" and seeing a whole new world, in a very different way.

Key Learnings:

- ✓ Being attentive will allow you to connect with more potential clients.
- ✓ Being attentive will develop and enhance relationships.

passionate. attentive. VOCAL. exceptional

What Will I Learn?

- How to attract multiple clients in a very short time.
- How to be heard.

Your voice needs to be heard. Using your voice is a very efficient way to share your passion and your services. I'd recommend using your voice in as many ways as possible, to target visual, auditory, and kinaesthetic preferences. Some people love to read, others love to listen, and others simply prefer to feel. Ensuring that your voice appeals to all preferences, will allow you to really connect with a multitude of people.

To win clients, you need to focus on being heard through:

1. Spoken words.
2. Written words.

If few people are aware of your services, then you will struggle to win clients. Businesses are lost in whispers of 'I'm here'. My advice is to turn up the volume. Seriously. Raise it up so high so that the world cannot help but hear you! People need to know about who you are and what you can do. You are serving. You owe it to the world to share your voice.

Raising Your Volume Through Spoken Word

Learning to present powerfully is the secret to raising your volume through spoken word. If the thought of speaking in public fills you with dread, then you are not alone. Glossophobia is very, very common, but you can and should overcome this fear. I know it's possible, because I did it, and it was the best investment that I ever made. My first, tiny, three-minute-long presentation resulted in my whole body shaking. I wondered if I was having a seizure – seriously! I now stand in front of large audiences on a regular basis, and not only speak with supreme confidence, but thrive on public speaking. Not only that, I teach other coaches and mentors to do the same. Presenting powerfully is all about skill acquisition; when you develop the skills, you will focus on your audience, not on your fear. Fear disappears and is replaced with excitement. You can learn to not only like public speaking, but to love it. When you love it, so will your audience. They will warm to you and want to work with you. Speaking to an audience, you will pave the way for not just one, but many potential clients.

Presenting Powerfully Wins Hearts. Winning Hearts Wins Clients

In a very short space of time, you can deliver a presentation that targets people with visual, auditory, and kinaesthetic preferences, rapidly and with power. Using visual aids, such as flip charts or props, you will target **visual** people. Using your voice and words, you will appeal to those who like to learn through **listening**. By using skills such as stage anchoring (eliciting emotional states within the audience using stage space) you can encourage people to **feel**. You will be heard, and I mean **really** heard and remembered by many. With a strong call to action at the end of a presentation, you can win immediate clients. You will P.A.V.E the way for many. Furthermore, do not underestimate the long-term impact of a presentation. You may well receive enquiries from potential clients many months and sometimes years after a presentation – simply because you made an impact and they remembered you.

My top tip is to be unafraid to share your own personal story. If you want to win clients, then you need to give them confidence in you. They need to see you "walking your talk". Nothing will give them more confidence than hearing you share your own personal journey. Your audience will love to know why you do what you do. If you want to take your clients from where they are to where they want to be, then make it clear that you are a personal expert in this field. Sharing your story will help you to do this.

I've listened to many excuses over the years from various solopreneurs, all trying desperately to avoid sharing their story and their truth:

- 'No-one will want to listen.'
- 'People will think I'm arrogant.'
- 'My story isn't interesting enough.'

You can choose to hold onto similar beliefs. Or you can ditch them, right now, and change them to:

- 'My story is unique, and people will enjoy it.'
- 'I can be confident without being arrogant.'
- 'My story needs to be heard. This is not about me. It's about them. By not providing them with the inspiration that they need, I am denying them the chance to change and improve their lives.'

Now, ask yourself the following questions:

Q What have you believed about your story?

Q What could you choose to believe instead?

STOP THE EXCUSES AND STEP UP!

My advice to you is to learn to present powerfully. Then seek out audiences to share your presentations with. Search for community groups or organisations that may be looking for speakers. Never exclude groups just because you feel that they may not be your clientele. Many years ago, I was asked to give a talk to a group of very elderly people who gathered once a week for a meal cooked by the local community. I nearly said no, thinking, 'Why would 80 and 90-year-olds want to hear about personal development?' My assumption was that they could probably teach me a thing or two with their life experiences. However, curiosity as to how I would be received got the better of me, and I said yes – fortunately. At the end of the presentation, a 90-year-old man hobbled up to me on his walking frame. He threw his arms around me, with tears pouring down his face, and said through sobs, 'Thank you. My whole life has suddenly made sense.' If that wasn't enough, one of the cooks then asked for my card and became a client. Never presume that audiences will not be interested. You could not only be losing clients but missing out on beautiful experiences.

I recommend speaking as often as possible, to as many different people as possible. Some may pay; others simply haven't got the resources. Do it anyway. It will come back tenfold.

Raising Your Volume Through Written Word

Combining spoken words with written words, to promote your business and win clients, is essential. Doing this will provide you with maximum exposure, and therefore increased opportunities to win and keep clients. There are many ways to maximise your opportunities using the written word. The ways that I've found most useful are as follows:

Use Social Media to Share Content

Ensure that your voice is heard on a regular basis on social media. Don't just share the posts of other experts. Show that you yourself are an expert, and share your knowledge. Use everyday experiences to create content. If you find yourself inspired by an experience, then share, adding suggested tools or ideas for the reader. Never underestimate simplicity; some of the simplest stories are the most powerful. Powerful posts that touch hearts will be shared, and this is especially the case if you have a strong call to action. Reply to comments and create conversations. Don't be afraid to be different, or express beneficial opinions. Overcome the fear of being wrong, or the fear of judgement, because worrying about what others will think will squash not only you, but your authenticity. So, speak your truth, and be a leader. Say what others are afraid to say. Be the light that they want to follow.

Use Twitter to Connect with Journalists and Create Media Opportunities

If you don't use Twitter, then start. It took me a long time to appreciate Twitter. At first, I found it abrupt and impersonal. However, when I learnt to use it effectively, I began to see fantastic results. As a result, my business has been featured in national newspapers and magazines. Sometimes my own written word is featured, and at other times I provide content, and the articles are written about me, for me. Use journalist request services to source daily opportunities. (I'd recommend www.journorequest.com). Focus on creating exposure, so that you are visible for potential clients.

Build Relationships with Your Local Journalists

Journalists are busy people. They are constantly sourcing new content. Why not make life easier for them, and provide content? Write your own articles and email them to newspapers or magazines. If you are running a workshop or event, let them know about it and invite them along. Alternatively, search the worldwide web for specific national or international days/events. Examples include:

- ⌘ International Day of Happiness (20th March).
- ⌘ World Kindness Day (13th November).
- ⌘ National Compliment Day (24th January).
- ⌘ Love Your Red Hair Day! (5th November).

Find a day that could be applicable to your business, and then write an article that could either help or educate the reader. Send your article to the appropriate people, and if they like it, they may well use it. Not only will you benefit from the business exposure, but you will also increase your credibility as an expert in your field.

Write for National Magazines

If you have a story, an opinion to express, or knowledge to share that relates to your business, then write for and send articles to national magazines. Do your research and look for magazines that may be interested in your content. If you don't hear anything back, don't take it personally. You may not get a reply. But if you keep doing it often enough, there is a good chance that you will get a positive response. Being featured in such a publication is a huge boost for business, because it demonstrates your expertise and again increases credibility.

Seek Out Industry Specific Opportunities

You may also have great success in writing specifically for industries. Are there organisations that send out regular newsletters, for which your content may be useful? Are there professional bodies that are always looking for fresh content? Could you write a guest blog for another professional?

Write down a list of all the possible ways that you could share your written knowledge using audiences that already exist. Keep this list and add to it frequently. Don't wait to be asked to write for them, just do it and send it. Ensure that all communication is friendly, warm, and inviting! It's totally possible to connect with a heart through an email!

Key Learnings:

- ✓ Focus on communicating through both spoken and written word.
- ✓ Learning to present powerfully is an essential investment.
- ✓ Find audiences that already exist.

passionate. attentive. vocal. EXCEPTIONAL

What Will I Learn?

- Why you need to be exceptional.
- How you can be exceptional.

You can be vanilla. There's nothing wrong with vanilla. But it's far better to be the triple flavour ice-cream, offering a variety of textures, covered in chocolate sauce and sprinkles, finished off with a flake and a cherry on top. (That's how a colleague described me once as a coach, and it warmed my heart.)

I urge you to be a unique blend of flavours. I urge you to be so tasty, that once a client has experienced you, they will tell the world about you. It's fun, it makes people feel special, and it creates wonderful experiences. By being exceptional, you will be memorable. Be exceptional "from your heart". Create wonderful experiences for your current clients, and you will not only keep them short-term, but potentially forever.

Here are some recommended steps to ensure that you too, are exceptional:

Overdeliver

Overdeliver. Seriously overdeliver. Give people what they need, and more. And more again. Go above and beyond, exceeding their expectations. If applicable, keep a record of their progress so that you can remind them of what they have achieved by working with you. Don't just give them an experience. Give them one of the most profound and powerful experiences of their life. When emotions attach to memories, they stay strong. By overdelivering, you ensure that your clients will feel strong and positive emotions. Be the person that they still talk about in 2 years, 10 years, and for the rest of their life.

Listen and Ask Outside

Focus and listen intensely. Have you ever witnessed a couple having a romantic dinner together, so wrapped up in each other that the world around them almost ceases to exist? This is what you need to aim for (minus the romance and the roses). Listen deeply to your client and their words. Within their words are the clues that will help you serve them best. Listen to what they need, so that you can give them exactly what they want, and more.

In addition, "ask outside". By this, I mean ask about the person, and their life beyond the business conversation. Show interest in their family and their friends. Find out what they like, and what they love. Allow a little extra time between client appointments, enabling you to do this. It's better to have fewer clients that you can spend extra time with, than many clients who feel rushed.

Tell Their Truth

If the client can't see their potential, then be bold and show them. Be unafraid to share your observations. If you spot something special within them, tell them. Open their eyes to the truth. When you see it, say it. Dare to say what most people never say. You will experience a connection with your client in that moment, which is hard to put into words. You can start by practising this at a lighter level, complimenting strangers on their perfume, clothing, or eye colour. Always ensure that your compliments are genuine and from the heart. Notice how you make them feel. This will help you to understand the potential power of your words and your presence.

Post a Surprise

Post small gifts that have great meaning for your client. If your client wants to be more courageous, and you have discussed the courage of a lion, then post them a toy lion! Send flowers by post. Or send a book that they may benefit from reading. Ask yourself, 'What would my client need or love?' Thinking of your clients when they least expect you to be thinking of them will create beautiful memories for you both. As an example, a friend of mine was on the telephone to a mobile phone company, when she happened to mention that it was her birthday the next day. Low and behold, she received a very cute little box of chocolates the next day, with a small handwritten note from the person who took her call. She still talks to people about this five years later. How do you think people perceive this company when they hear her story?

"I've learned that people will forget what you said, people will forget what you did, but people will never forget how you made them feel." – Mary Angelou

Remember Key Dates

If your client has a personal event coming up, then drop them a text or an email wishing them good luck. Let them know that you are thinking about them. Send them a birthday card or a wedding gift. Send a card for no other reason than to tell them how much you believe in them or appreciate them. Think of the most amazing thing that you could do for them, and do it. It's the thought that counts, but it's what you do with that thought that really matters.

Polish Your Treasures

Keep in contact with as many clients as possible. Polish your treasures. Drop old clients an email, asking them about their progress. Show that you genuinely care about them. You will be amazed at how much repeat business this brings. Doing this reminds your clients that you are still there for them if they need you. Be genuinely interested in their progress and lives. Continue to celebrate their ongoing achievements with them whenever possible. Be the first person they think of when they need your service. If I see an opportunity for a client, even after they have finished working with me, I will always send them details. It takes less than a minute to send an email, but could create an opportunity for a client which will last a lifetime. I'm a firm believer in continuing to go the extra mile.

Be a Rule Breaker

Bend the rules, and don't be afraid to break them. The most successful solopreneurs are the most flexible. In the early days, you may try to conform, sticking rigidly to tools, techniques, and processes. This will limit your results and your clients. Don't give them what the textbooks say they need – give them what they really need! Use your intuition. Unleash your creativity and develop your own strategies to use. Sometimes the crazy stuff makes the biggest difference. I've stood in a heavy downpour helping clients "wash away" their limiting beliefs. We've thrown their written traumas into burning flames, and sat on rollercoasters together to help them overcome fears.

Be a Connector and a Creator

Connect and create opportunities for your clients. Being a solopreneur gives us great freedom. Unrestricted by rules, we can do what we want, when we want. With their individual permissions, I have connected many clients, for the benefit of both parties. This has been known to benefit businesses, and even led to romantic relationships! Create opportunities for your clients to grow, by helping them to help each other.

Believe in Your Client

Believe that every single client can live a rich, fulfilling, and happy life. There will be clients that test you, clients that challenge you, and clients that resist you. Refuse to back down. Understand the reasons for their behaviour. Be consistent in your approach and commitment. Make it clear that you will not give up on them, and that you are totally committed to their needs and desired outcomes.

Be Unafraid of Your Own Emotions

It's likely that both you and your client will experience several powerful emotions whilst working together. Never be afraid of showing your emotions. There will be moments when you will need to be strong, but it can also be beneficial to allow your emotions to show. There have been times when I've spotted the most incredible strengths and skills within a client, whilst they are oblivious to these. I've sat with obvious tears in my eyes, and asked them if they know how inspiring and amazing they are. These are always profoundly powerful moments for us both. Following such an experience, clients often comment on how amazing these sessions are. To this day, I'm still reduced to a crumpled wreck whenever a client reaches the end of their programme and tells me how I've either saved or changed their life. And yes, we often hug too. Because as solopreneurs, we can. Showing vulnerability allows our authenticity to shine through. It shows them that we really, really care.

Key Learnings:

- ✓ Being exceptional will make people feel special.
- ✓ Being exceptional will win and keep many clients.
- ✓ It's okay to break rules, in order to be exceptional.

Obstacle Obliteration

What Will I Learn?

- That obstacles will appear.
- Why collaboration is better than competition.
- Failure does not exist.

Being **P**assionate, **A**ttentive, **V**ocal and **E**xceptional will ensure that you are a successful solopreneur. Being strong in all four of these disciplines will enable you to acquire and retain clients. As you P.A.V.E the way, however, obstacles may appear! Knowing about potential obstacles, will allow you to deal with such things ahead of time. Knowledge is power. Knowledge will enable you to identify obstacles and move past them! Compare obstacles to boulders blocking your path. You can choose to stop and give up (but not on my watch!) or find a way around them, to continue serving and changing the world.

There are two potential obstacles that many solopreneurs experience:

1. Perceived competition.
2. Perceived failure.

When you find yourself facing either of these two obstacles, it may appear that they are caused by external circumstances. This is not true. Understanding this is essential. Competition and failure are not caused by external circumstances, but by our thoughts and perceptions. When we take responsibility for the creation of our own "boulders", we either demolish or find a way around them! Always take full responsibility for your creation. Ask yourself, 'What am I thinking or believing, that has created this obstacle?'

The following words will help you to challenge your thoughts and perceptions. They will help you to take full responsibility for your obstacles, and help you remove them rapidly and with ease.

Collaboration Not Competition

'It's getting harder to find clients, because there is so much competition out there.'

I've heard this statement a few times, usually spilled from the lips of newer solopreneurs. If you have uttered these words yourself, then go grab a pen, the darkest blackest most permanent pen that you can find. Draw a line through that statement. Don't worry about "messing up" this book; it's your book, for your use. Do what you need to do. Be bold and brave.

The truth is, it's not hard to find clients. And there is no competition. These beliefs are just stories that you have made up about your circumstances, to help you justify your perceived failures. Note the word "perceived". Sometimes it's easier to blame external circumstances, than change ourselves. Never take the easy path. Decide to keep changing yourself, until you find yourself winning and keeping clients.

There is no competition, because there is no other you. Understand that there never can be any competition, because:

- You are unique. Within your brain there are countless networks of neural pathways formed by your life, learnings, and experiences. No-one has the same neural network as you; therefore, no-one can be like you. No-one can deliver like you. You cannot compare yourself to others.
- There are different strokes for different folks. Some clients may be very suited to you; others may be more suited to another professional. Never work with a client because you must. Work with them because you want to.
- Training and certification do not make us all the same. We all use our knowledge in different ways. No-one can ever replicate your clients' experience, because you create your own client experience.

Ditch the idea of competition. Instead, embrace collaboration. Create a community of like-minded professionals, who unite through passion. Reach out to complete strangers in similar professions and ask to meet for a coffee. Create communities via Facebook groups. Strengthen these communities by facilitating group meet-ups. Offer support and advice to other professionals, and you yourself will receive support and advice in return.

As a solopreneur, it can become lonely, but only if you allow it to be. With this in mind, I urge you to create joint ventures, through which you can make a difference to people and the world. Ditching competition and seeking positive collaboration will prevent this from happening; there is nothing better than meeting with a group of passionate, like-minded individuals for a coffee! Your tribe will "get you", be there for you when you fall, and shout from the rooftops with you to celebrate your success.

Overcoming Perceived Failure

You will make mistakes, and in some way, you need to make these mistakes in order to learn. Experiencing the pain induced by your perceived failures is necessary. It's fundamental to creating clients, keeping them, and developing a successful business. Some solopreneurs fall at the first hurdle and never get up, deciding that their mistake means that they are not capable. So. Not. True.

Without perceived failure there can be no success. As a small child learning to walk, did you give up at the first fall? No. You tried and tried again, until you got it right. You need to fall, in order to fly. Here are a few of my personal perceived failures:

- Spending a very large sum of money on marketing that did not work (expensive).
- Experiencing "no show" clients (frustrating).
- Forgetting a client's name (cringe).
- Thinking that I could work endless hours with endless clients (burnout).
- Selling my story to a women's magazine, thinking it would promote my business. Instead they twisted my story to suit their trashy mag without a mention of my business (fortunately).
- Believing that my client's growth was my responsibility (never).

These are just **some** of the errors that I made in my early days of business. But boy, the pain that they induced made sure that I never, ever made those same mistakes again. And the lessons that I learnt as a result have proved invaluable.

You will make mistakes too. There will be days where you want to crawl into a hole and never be seen again. There will be days where you beat yourself black and blue with your words, as you feel "not good enough", or "not competent enough". But it's all part of the journey. Making mistakes **does not** mean that you will not be a success. Making mistakes means that you are **closer** to success. Always one step closer.

Everything that you get wrong, delivers valuable feedback to ensure that you won't experience the same again. When you've learnt how not to do it, you discover how to do it. Obliterate the word failure from your vocabulary and your life. Imagine a world without failure – then live in it, starting now. Do it for the clients that you have yet to meet. Do it for the people that need your services. Do it because the world needs you, and what you have to offer. You are here to serve. Dish it up.

Some solopreneurs give up at the first obstacle, but not you. You will overcome any challenge, because you know that the world needs you. You will get back up after a fall, because of your desire to make a difference. You will always find a way, to continue to P.A.V.E the way to success. Now, you see the bigger picture. You understand that it's not about you or them – it's about us all. It's about the changes that we can make individually, that combine to make the world a better place. It's about leading with our hearts to create authentic and rewarding relationships, which not only enhance our businesses, but our lives. When leading from the heart becomes our norm, client acquisition and retention becomes our norm too.

It's now time to take my words and own them. It's time to live with them and live by them. Knowing how to P.A.V.E the way, you are powerful. Knowing how to clear your path, you are unstoppable. Leading from your heart, you are memorable. Step into your power. Own your power. Use your power. Your clients are waiting.

Key Learnings:

- ✓ Obstacles are expected.
- ✓ Obstacles are created with your mind, and can therefore be changed by your mind.
- ✓ There is no failure, only feedback.

Biography

Life Changer Maria Hocking is an inspiring coach, captivating speaker, and author, who is passionate about changing lives with her heart and her words. Having overcome many personal challenges throughout her life, she is walking, talking proof that what she shares works.

Maria's message is clear, 'What happens to you does not define you, but helps you to find yourself.' Excelling in the field of personal development, she travels the world – coaching, speaking, and changing lives. Maria is also a highly regarded mentor for new coaches, and thrives on helping other professionals change the world too.

Maria can be reached via her website: www.mariahocking.com

CHAPTER SIX

by

Ruby McGuire

3 Fabulous Strategies to Create Your Dream Business

Hi, I'm Ruby, Business Mastery & Mindset Queen. I'm going to be sharing lots of things to help you get those fabulous clients that you dream of. I call them "dreamie" clients. Here's what's coming up:

1. A Fear to Fabulousness strategy. (A simple tool to help you move through fear.)
2. A model to help you create a visible and profitable business, including how to attract your "dreamie" clients with ease, and then how to keep them.
3. How to give back as part of your business model.

There are 3 things you need to crack, to bring in new clients:

1. **Your self-belief** – you need to believe you are good at what you do, and that you can help your clients.
2. **Your info** – you need to know who your clients are, where they are, and what you offer.
3. **Your skill** – you need to develop your skillset. I'll be sharing a template that you can use to help build your skill, then it's just about practising over and over again so that offering your services become natural.

You've probably heard time and time again that thoughts become your reality. So, if you feel poor, you'll attract less. If you feel you can never get clients, or can never get discovery calls, then you can guess what will happen. Set some intentions around what you're trying to achieve here. Just saying, 'I want more clients' isn't going to cut it. How many clients? What level of client? What kind of services would you like to offer?

Let me tell you a story…

Once upon a time, there was a service-based business owner. Let's call her Sally, for the purpose of this story. Sally's business wasn't going well. She worried all the time about how she was going to pay the bills. She was telling herself that she had to work hard to get new clients, that it was too challenging. She would huff and puff any time she had to work with new technology, and sales conversations were a whole new ordeal. Sally found the process of signing up new clients extremely painful, and was considering packing it in. Every time she had a "discovery call" it bombed. (A discovery call is a call you have with a potential client to find out what they need support with, to identify how you can help and to find out if you are a good fit to work together.) She kept on giving everything away, underselling her services, undercharging, and sometimes even working for free. The problem was that nobody was signing up to work with her. Sally always felt like there was never enough time to do all that she needed to do, and that she was taking two steps forward and one step back. She'd often tell herself she'd be better off giving up, and getting a "proper job", and found herself procrastinating on what to even do in her business, because whatever she did seemed to fail.

Sally had three main things holding her back in her business:

1. Her mindset wasn't serving her. She was spiralling into negativity, which was then having an impact on her business.
2. She needed to get a better understanding of who her "dreamie" clients were, and how she could help them.
3. She needed to work on some business skills – to learn how to market, how to sell, and how to have strong and powerful conversations.

The first step to creating a better mindset is to notice what you're telling yourself. To have a strong mindset, you need your language to empower you, not pull you down. Fear is one of the biggest things that come up when wanting to bring in new clients. "Selling" triggers all our fear buttons.

We're going to start by learning how to release all this fear. Let me introduce you to the Fear to Fabulousness strategy.

Part 1: Fear to Fabulousness Strategy

Think about your business. As you do so, write down any fears that come into your mind. For example: *I'm scared that/of...* These fears are all becoming "your story", and we want to create a much more fabulous story instead! Let it all out, honey – it's liberating! Be as negative as you want to be. We'll be moving on to clearing it all, next. Let's do some releasing of all that icky stuff!

I created an acronym for **F.E.A.R** over breakfast one morning, with my lovely hubby and daughter. The original seed of the idea came from my own coach, and then I expanded on it further. I was trying to come up with something that helped me to remember the best way to release all this rubbish, and while "Fear Dump" was a great method (where you "dump" all your fears out on paper), the name just didn't work for me. So, we got creative, and this is what we ended up with.

F for Feelings

E for Express

A for Acknowledge

R for Release

Let's walk through the process together. I'll explain how it works and then share an example.

F = Feelings

Choose one statement you made on the previous page, and then ask yourself what **feelings** are coming up for you, so that you can understand what might be beneath the statement. Do this for each statement in turn. It's one thing to think of what the feeling is. It's another thing to write it down/feel it.

Example:

Feeling: Mine used to be that you must work really hard to bring in money. That would bring up a feeling of anxiety in my tummy, it made me feel worried that I wouldn't be able to do the other things that I wanted to do.

Next, write down the feeling. If you can, recreate it. I often have to "think" into it, but I do know if I really think about the issue it does bring up a sensation/feeling for me.

E = Express

Now it's time to **express** those feelings. It's one thing writing them on paper, but I want you to give them a bit more power for a moment, by reading them out loud. Remember just to say one single statement at a time, not all in one go. It's important that we do the releasing of each one individually.

Example:

Express: 'I have to work really hard to bring in money.' Say your statement out loud. Give it some power, just for now.

A = Acknowledge

Feelings come up for a reason. They are our guiding system. We can be all "Pollyanna" about it and say we aren't going to let them happen, but that's not healthy. Healthy is about recognising and **acknowledging** feelings. We are allowed to feel how we feel. It's what we do with those feelings that matters.

Example:

Acknowledge: Say, 'Thank you for bringing this fear to my attention. I acknowledge you.' (Your monkey mind is just trying to protect you by bringing up this fear – that little nagging voice trying to protect you. They're often called monkeys; they're mischievous and cause havoc!) Acknowledge that this is how you feel. It's okay for you to feel this way.

R = Release

Yay! It's time to let it all go.

Example:

Release: Finally, it's time to release your fear. Say, 'I choose to release you now' and cross it off the list. You can even say 'Rubbish', or 'Nonsense', or whatever word works for you, to release any power the fear has over you. It's SO freeing!

Sometimes, the fear doesn't come back, but I've found that on occasions it will still be there. If this happens, then go through the process again and work through whatever comes up for you. If necessary, get someone, such as a coach, to help you release any limiting beliefs that might not be serving you.

Now that we've done a bit of fear clearing, we can get onto the fun step of creating your dream business. This is the pillar of everything that you do. If your mindset monkeys are acting up and running the show, it doesn't matter what you do, you're not going to get the same results as when you're feeling confident in what you do. The stories we tell ourselves are incredibly powerful. They can be the difference between getting clients and not, and the difference between having a super successful business, and just having a hobby. There are other authors in this book talking about mindset, therefore I won't spend more time on this. Check out Ali's chapter, where he shares his inspiring story from being a performance artist. The bit about taking a leap has really stuck with me!

Part 2: Let's Create a Fabulous, Visible and Profitable Business

Creating a dream business can be both exciting and challenging. Perhaps you're realising that your business is just an expensive hobby. You're not on your own. Lots of my clients have had this realisation. It's not necessarily all doom and gloom. Maybe you just don't have the right foundations. There are over 80,000 ways to market your business, and if you've bought into the online hype that you can build a successful business overnight, then it's no wonder you're feeling flat about your exciting dream not having come to fruition yet. Let's go back to basics, so that you can turn that idea of a dream business into a reality, step by step. After all, you're in business, and that's what it's all about, right? But how can it be so hard? Well it doesn't have to be. If you want to get visible and profitable then it's all about connection.

Now, we'll explore the 5 steps to creating a visible and profitable business. It's time to connect with your:

1. Passion
2. Dreamies
3. Offering
4. Message
5. Tribe

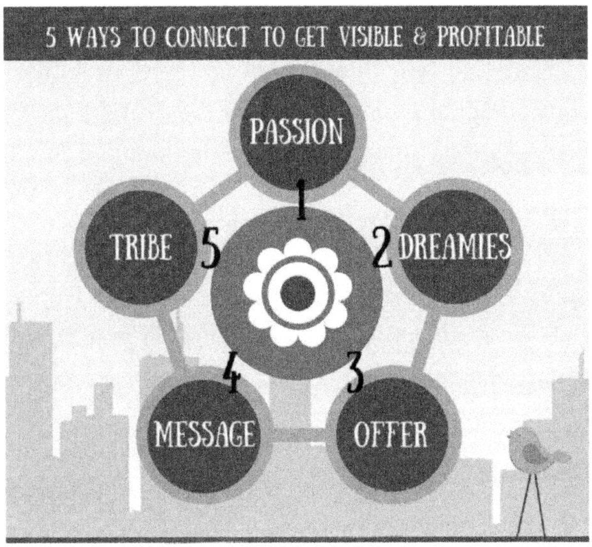

1. Passion

In order to connect with your people, you need to explore what you're passionate about. As a business owner, it's likely you already know what you've been called to do. However, it might also still feel a bit messy in your head, like tangled spaghetti that needs unknotting. When running a business, you'll need to put a lot of effort in, so you want your passion to drive you for those days when it feels like hard work. Once you know what that passion is, your message will be clearer, whether that's online or in person.

In business, you need to know your big "why". Why have you chosen this area of business? Why is this important to you? Your "why" will drive you to achieve. It will motivate you to act. If you're not driven by your passion, it could become a struggle to get out of bed and run your business. It will also be evident in all that you do, as the energy you put out there will be different. We can all tell when someone's "just in it for the money", right?

Action: Get absolute clarity around what you want to do. When running a business, this is something that can often be overlooked. Write a list of all the things that truly light you up, and what you're passionate about. Figure out your big "why". Why are you doing this? If you had all the money you needed, and that wasn't your driving force, what would you do businesswise?

2. Dreamies

The next step is to figure out who your "dreamie" clients are. Ask yourself the following question: who are the people that you'd love to work with? Think about past clients that you've worked with, and how they lit you up. Why was this? Think about what you know about your potential clients, and who they might be. What could they be struggling with? What might be going on for them in their daily lives?

Action: Write down all the things you love about the people you've worked with so far (in business or in your personal life). Consider things like their personality, the things they were interested in, the way they think etc. Once you've worked out your passion and your "dreamies", the next step is to work out what you are going to offer them. You need to get absolute clarity on your services, and help people connect with them as quickly as possible.

3. Offer

If you're confident in what you're offering, clients are much more likely to buy from you – because they'll feel confident in you and know that you can help them. Self-confidence projects, it means that when you're putting your services out there and making your business visible to the world, people will remember you for the right reasons. You'll be seen as the go-to person in your area of business. I often hear people say, 'Charge what you're worth'. I don't buy into that, because if you don't get clients signing up with you because of price, your little mindset monkey may act up – equating that with you being worthless. I say charge what your **services** are worth instead. When you're creating your offerings, you don't need to throw in everything. Your clients don't need your grandma or your goldfish!

Action:

Spend some time doing some market research with clients/potential clients to find out what support they need. Hold lots of connection calls to ask them; you don't need to guess. As you get clarity from the calls, it will be so much easier to figure out the kind of content that you want to offer. If you'd like some help with pricing and a template of what you could say, check out my section in our workbook, which accompanies this book.

4. Message

Once you know you're doing what you love (Passion), have figured out who you love working with (Dreamies), and know what you're offering (Offers), it's time to get your message out there.

This can often be the place where people get a bit stuck, because fear gets in the way. You may have a big message to share, but your inner voice is telling you that you're not good enough to shout about what you do. It's saying, *'What will people think of you?'* or *'What if you say the wrong thing and someone doesn't like you or your content?'* I get it. Personally, I hate confrontation and feel physically sick when I mess things up, but I know that my message is bigger than my fear, so I just share and trust that the right people will get my message. If my message resonates with them, then they are part of my tribe. If not, I'm simply not the right one for them. We can't be all things to all people.

With the above in mind – be you. If you want people to connect with you, then share your personal story, share your vulnerabilities, your mess-ups. All the things that have been part of your journey to where you are now are key – your background, experience, and expertise. Show up 100% as you, and that will help you to stand out from the crowd. Own your uniqueness. It doesn't matter how many businesses there are in the same market as you, YOU are what makes your business different. Nobody can do you like you can.

Let's be honest, running a business can be hard. We all have our doubts and things that can hold us back, so work on your mindset. To truly connect with people, you need to come from a place of service – not fear, panic, or worry. Surround yourself with support, meditate, and write a gratitude list – a list of all that you're grateful for; work with someone to help you get over any limiting beliefs that might be holding you back. Do whatever it takes to feel more confident. It's important to remember too that you are not the only person with fear and self-doubt. It happens to all of us, from time to time. From my experience, once you accept that these emotions are normal, and not a sign of failure, it will become easier to remove your own blocks, and the feeling of being "stuck".

Action:

Write down 12 main topics that you know loads about. Split those 12 topics into 4 sub-topics. You then have 48 topics (nearly a year's worth of content titles that you can then explore and expand on).

Think about stories that you could tell about you, with a little twist to help connect with your "dreamies". Let's say I share a story about something I'm proud of. At the end of the post, I turn it back to my clients to share something about them that they're proud of too. It's all about encouraging, motivating, and inspiring your "dreamies". They will connect with you on a much deeper level when you share some of your own vulnerabilities.

5. Tribe

Although this is the last of my 5 connections, I believe this is the one that makes the single biggest difference in business. It's about connecting with your tribe, whether that's 1:1 or in any online/offline groups that you're in.

One way to build your tribe is to reach out to past and current clients, or business and personal connections, to have conversations. In those conversations, you can share what you're doing. I want you to know that even if you don't have clarity on who you want to work with or how you'll help them ...YET (make that your new phrase by the way because if you're working on it, then the inspiration will come!) you can still be connecting with people on a personal level. Just chat to people. By learning about others, you'll also learn lots about yourself too.

Having built relationships over the last few years, I have been able to reach out to lots of lovely people to invite them to join my programme. These clients have come from all sorts of places – local networking, online networking, via social media platforms, and even from within the local community. You can connect with people anywhere and everywhere. There was no pressure, no ickiness (discomfort), just an invite to talk to me about whether they would be a good fit or not. I've had amazing results – I achieved an 86% sign up on one programme I ran, and that's been common across the programmes I've run since. I put that down to my invitation being the right thing for the right people, and me having built relationships with the people I chose to speak to first. So, never underestimate the power of a simple conversation. Think about your own circumstances. Who could you have a conversation with today, not for business, but just to connect for fun? When you've answered this question – reach out :).

So, there you have it – 5 ways to connect with others, in order to help you grow your dream business. Which one will you start with? Spend some time figuring this one out. Then, once you have that nailed, you can move onto the next stage of creating your "dreamie" clients with ease.

Stop reading now – it's time to do some work! Go back through those last steps and work on steps 1-3 before you read another word. Don't just read – DO the work. That means you'll already be on the way to creating your dream business, with paying clients!

I mean it.

Stop reading.

Not a single word more.

Simple Process to Attract "Dreamie" Clients with Ease

Now that you have clarity on your passion, "dreamies", and offering, you can start to implement a simple process now for attracting "dreamie" clients with ease. It doesn't have to be hard work, but you do need a strategy. It's time for you to start connecting with your beautiful "dreamies".

This work could bring up a lot of fear, procrastination and self-doubt. Work on releasing those fears.

You've got the Fear to Fabulousness strategy now, so you can use that daily – to bust all those fears. They don't serve you, and they certainly won't help you run a successful business. You need to step into the powerful business owner persona, not the one that's just got an expensive hobby. To reduce some of your fear of reaching out to people, I want you to do a simple reframe.

The best way to build a business is by connecting with people. Connection is SO underrated these days. It accounts for a huge percentage of my business, about 85-90% in fact. Traditional selling sucks! You'll of heard many people talk about the "know-like-trust" that's required for people to buy, and it's true. When you come from a place of "selling" it can feel extremely uncomfortable. On the other hand, when you come from a place of offering your services, and you have the intention that you're reaching out to build relationships, a lot of fear can be removed. You simply want to find out if you can even help that person, and if you can, then you can invite them to take the next step with you, whatever that next step is.

It's easy to get caught up in the mindset that simply talking to people about working with them is hard selling. But this is a myth. You didn't set up in business to be a sleazy salesperson, and you don't have to be one. I'm sure you'll have set up your business to make a difference, to help people and support them. You're not that sleazy salesperson, so you can rest knowing that it's highly unlikely you're going to turn into one overnight! Work on YOU. Know WHY you're scared of inviting people to work with you. For most people, this is down to fear of failure, fear of rejection, or fear of judgement. They ask themselves questions like:

- 'What will my friends think of me promoting what I do?'
- 'What will my work colleagues say about me?'
- 'What if I fall flat on my face?'
- 'What if I mess up and people start talking about my failures?'

You can see here, there's a lot of "What ifs?", and a lot of fear! Well, **what if** they love what you do, and say amazing things about you? **What if** you do an incredible job? Allow yourself to consider these things, as we move into the next section.

Personally, I think that if you have no conversations with people, then you're not in business. You're letting people down. By not offering your services, they won't know how you can help them – you'll just be the world's best-kept secret. That's not helpful to your potential "dreamie" clients, nor is it helpful for your bank balance.

One of the things I used to do when I started out, was to set so much expectation on the call. I wanted that one client to sign up, and thought that if they didn't then I was a complete failure. Little did I know that it wasn't that they didn't want to buy from me, it was that I was offering everything to them, overwhelming them and coming across as desperate. All that does is send out needy energy. You're putting a crazy amount of pressure on you, that call, and that person, for them to become your "dreamie" client. So, drop that need. Detach yourself from the outcome. Remember, you're coming from a place of service. Once you do that, you'll find that things start to shift. Instead of throwing everything at them, you'll start to relax and find out what that client really needs help with. It's scary, but you need to trust that if they are meant to be your client, they will come your way. You may have 10 calls and none of those people sign up. Yet they may come back later, or they may know someone else that they recommend you to.

Reach out to others, and know that the one client you're so intent on signing up isn't the only one that could be a good fit for you. Have the call, go and do something fun afterwards, and let them decide if they are right for you or not.

You then need to CHOOSE. You need to DECIDE that bringing in clients is easy. Your brain will then go on a search to find out how you can bring them in with ease. If you speak to most super successful business owners, and ask them how they turned their business around, it's often the case that they made the decision for their business to be successful, and then took the action to make that happen.

Let's break down some of the beliefs that might be holding you back from "selling", and challenge them:

'I'm too expensive. They will never pay that!' Compared to whom? How do you know? Would you pay that? If not, you need to consider what needs to change so that you can believe in what you're selling! What's the return on investment of them working with you? Whenever you are working on your pricing, consider what value you can add, and what outcomes they will get as a result of working with you. How can you add value so that it feels more in alignment with you?

Remember, some people will pay £25 for coaching/other services, whereas others will pay £10,000 – it's all relative, and not about the number, but the perceived value. Like anything in business, services range from low-end to high-end.

Let's take shoes as an example. You can get a cheap £20/$25 pair of shoes, or you can buy Christian Louboutin for £500/$550 and beyond. Now, I know there's the phrase that says, 'Cinderella is proof that a new pair of shoes can change a girl's life', but so can your services! Everyone has their thing, and that's what I mean here. Some people want to pay budget prices; some people like to pay for the best of the best, with high-end experiences. **You** get to choose what level you want to work at, and charge accordingly. 'But I don't want to be salesy,' I hear you say. Of course, you don't. Your potential clients don't want you to either. Remember, if you're coming from a place of service, you're just helping them to decide – that's it!

Know the benefits of working with you – the **transformation** that you bring. Base your prices on that. You'll find it a lot easier to share what you do, and translate your message into conversions.

'I don't know what to say.' Add the word 'yet' onto the end of that sentence. I don't know what to say, yet. That's okay – you can learn!

'I undercharge all the time.' There is often a maximum ceiling on 1:1 work, where time can be a limiting factor for how many clients you can accommodate. Instead of trying to discount your services, think about how you can add value to your services, which will, in turn, enable you to increase your price point. The bigger issue here that needs addressing though, is why you're undercharging. Go back through the F.E.A.R model and work that one through, so that you clear the fear you have around selling your services.

'I over-deliver.' This one is SOOOO common! I still have to remind myself not to do this. You're not serving your client; they are only getting a percentage of what you can offer. You're overwhelming them with too much information, and they will get stuck again quickly.

'I feel like a fraud – I'm not as far ahead as my clients might think.' Can you help them? That's all it comes down to. If you can help your customers to achieve the results they desire, you don't need to be a million steps ahead of them. In fact, I'd add that if you're too far ahead then you're more likely to be out of touch with what they need, as you're too far removed from the challenges they are facing. There's a note to add here though – this isn't about exaggerating what you can offer. It's always better to exceed their expectations through your work.

'What if I can't get them the results?' This is another common one. If you genuinely don't think you can get the results, then create a different offering. However, if you think you can, but have some self-doubt, then it's likely that there's some unhealthy, limiting beliefs holding you back. The good news is, you can work on those. Work on improving your mindset before you go into the calls/conversations.

So, how do you even get to the point where you can persuade someone to have a call with you? Well, the simple, but not always easy thing to do, is simply invite them. Here's a list of some of the 101 ways that you could create connections with your potential "dreamies". Let's get your creative juices flowing:

- *Free discovery call, consultation, etc*

Invite people onto a call, to talk about how you might be able to help them. All you need here is a quick call where you can ask what they are struggling with, assess how you can help, and then explain the ways in which you can provide support.

- *Free taster session – strategy/discovery/relevant to your business*

This is similar to the discovery call, but this one is more about showcasing what you do. At the end of the call you can ask if they'd like to find out more about how to work with you. You can also do a mini action-plan, as part of the call, which will give you more chance to follow up.

- *Client interviews/surveys – 10 questions (FAB for newbies)*

This is a fabulous place to start if you don't know who your "dreamie" clients are, or you just want to understand them better. Offer the client interview – where you ask about 10-15 questions that will help you understand them better – and then offer them a free taster session in return. Questions could be something like, 'What are the main challenges you're facing?' or 'What would you say is stopping you from achieving your goals?' Again, great for follow-up too, as you can check in on their progress after the session.

- *Hold a webinar* – teach what you know; invite people onto a call with you at the end. This is a great way to build your list, gain credibility, and find opportunities for booking discovery calls. If the people watching the webinar like your content, they will want to find out more.
- *Share great content* – something that MUST not be overlooked. You must make sure you have great content (Step 5 of the Connection Plan – Connect with your Tribe). This will underpin what you do, help you to connect with your "dreamie" clients, and then make them want to talk to you. You can also pop a call to action on your posts. **Note**: I'd say do this with caution, as it's much more compelling if there is a time limit on your discovery calls.
- *Other people's groups* – often groups will hold marketing days; this is your chance to invite people to connect with you. What I would say here is make it more of a taster session for these than a discovery call, as you're more likely to get interest.
- *Group chats/networking* – be brave with conversations. Just chat away in groups/ network, and then if you think you can help that person, simply invite them onto a call with you.

Other things to try:

- *Invite onto a call* – as an add-on to group programmes, this is a great way to help people that you only know in a group capacity, and a fantastic opportunity to offer them more 1:1 work.
- *Speaking gigs* – make your call to action an invite to talk to you. Give clients the chance to find out how you can help them.
- *Referrals / affiliates* – invite onto a call as above, to talk about how you can help.
- *Email list* – set a maximum number of clients you want to work with; invite people that are serious about working with you onto a call. Explain who it's for and who it isn't – i.e. 'It's not for you if you aren't ready to invest in working with me.'

Okay so you've got them on the call, now what?

Let's quickly go through the discovery call process. You may already know and do all of this, but in case you don't, here's a few pointers:

1. Set your intention. What would you like them to get out of the call?

2. Pre-frame the call. At the beginning of the call, you need to pre-frame what's going to happen over the next few minutes. Know where the clients are at, before you make the call. Do they know this is a sales call? If so, then make it clear that the purpose of the call is to find out if you're a good fit together. If it's just a taster session, or there has been no conversation about you working together, then simply tell them what it is you do and how you help people. At the end of the call, ask them if they'd like to know more. Assuming the answer is yes, you can then invite them onto another call, where you can explain how you'll help them **specifically.** At all times, keep it relaxed and conversational.

3. Take them on a journey of possibility

Listen carefully to what's going on for your clients, and take good notes, so that you can refer to them throughout the call. On the call you want to build the client's confidence in themselves, and their confidence in you. Use their language, and build great rapport with them. Find out what they want to create, so that you can help them to think big. They might not sign up with you, but if you can help them to step into a new place of possibility then this could be life-changing for them, whether they become a client or not.

4. Current challenges

You then want to talk about the client's current challenges. This is important to explore, as it will help you decide what to offer them.

5. Urgency/commitment

You then need to find out how urgent the problem is, and what their level of commitment is to resolve it and work with someone like you. If there's no urgency or commitment, then it's unlikely they are going to be committed to the process.

6. How you work

Explain how you work. Are you someone that likes to kick butt, or is your style more nurturing? Share this with them; it will help them to know if you're the right person to work with. If you're not a good fit for each other, you can both choose to end the call there and then.

7. Share case studies/explain how you help

Now that you know what the client's challenges are, you're able to share with them how you can help them overcome their problems. Perhaps you've worked with clients that have had similar problems. If you don't think they need your help, tell them. If you don't want to work with them, tell them. Of course, that one always feels a bit awkward, so make sure you do this the right way. Simply say that, having chatted things through with them, you've realised you're not the best fit for them, and if you are able to, recommend someone that would be.

Before you even explain the package, check in with the client to be sure you're the right fit. Talk to them about the package that's the best fit for them.

8. Explain the benefits of the programme

Go through the programme with them, the benefits, how it works, and the kind of results they can expect. Now it's time for them to throw their objections at you! Don't fear objections – they are good. When the client shares any objections with you, you can help overcome them while they are on the call. It's much better that they tell you about these objections, than ending the call and you never hearing from them again. It's sometimes a good idea to get the client to think the call over, ideally on the phone – that way you won't end up with clients feeling buyer's remorse/regretting signing up with you, and you can use this as an opportunity to dispel any doubts that they might have.

9. Help them decide

Support your clients through their self-doubt, fears, or money issues, and resolve these on the call. Here are some of the most common objections that come up, and how to deal with them:

- **'I'm not sure if it's right for me'** – this usually means that you haven't explained yourself well enough, and the client doesn't understand what it is they will get by working with you. Ask them what's coming up for them.
- **'I don't have enough time'** – this goes back to urgency and commitment. Ask them, 'How important is it that you fix this now?', 'What difference will it make to you if you fix this?' and/or 'What is the impact/benefit of doing nothing?' Remind them of what they've said about their challenges, and the impact these are having on them.
- **'I don't have the money'** – ask your client: 'If money weren't an option, would I still be the right fit for you?' If they say that you would, then check in on the kind of budget they have, and share with them how you might be able to help them at a lower price level. Maybe it's just a case of removing a few different added value items from your package, to reduce the overall price point. It could be a simple fix. Ask them what else they need from you, to help them decide. They may need time to think, but where possible get them to do their thinking on the call.

10. Give them a window of opportunity to decide

Ask the client how long they think they will need, in order to decide on whether they want to work with you or not. Invite them onto another call to finalise the process. Tell them it will be a quick 10-minute call, where they can ask any additional questions. Book the call, where possible, while they are with you. The worst case is they will cancel the call; the best case is they will make a quick decision.

I personally offer a fast-acting bonus for signing up within 48 hours of our call. It's always something of high value – ranging between £197 to £1497, depending on what level of package they are signing up for with me. This helps them to make a quick decision, and it's also lovely to be able to gift something extra to them.

So, are you going to be a selling machine at the end of doing all this? Initially, probably not. Over time you will find that you will get more and more conversions, as you start to hone what you say. You'll find out what works and what doesn't work for you, and it will all start to feel more natural.

You'll make loads of mistakes along the way. You'll probably still give away your grandmother, your house, and your goldfish as part of the process, but as time goes on, you'll feel more confident in what you're offering, and you'll stick with just offering your services, and not selling your soul too!

One thing that can help you with this is to get an accountability buddy, who you can test your sales conversations with. That's how I perfected (I say "perfected", on every single call you'll learn a better way of doing it next time) my own style, and it helped to get constructive feedback on how well I was doing and whether people would buy the service I was offering.

Now Comes the Consistency Piece – Keeping in Touch

So, you've got the clients coming in. Now you need to keep them, and for those that aren't your clients (yet) you want to keep in touch with them too. Your follow-up process doesn't have to be complicated.

Are You Leaving Money on the Table?

One question you need to ask yourself is whether you're leaving money on the table. You are if you're not…

- Following up – when did you last follow-up with potential clients that have shown an interest in what you do?
- Connecting with past clients – you may have a whole list of people you could reach out to today to offer your services, or simply to continue a conversation.

- Asking for referrals – who do you know that knows…?
- Reaching out to someone when you think your new service/offering will be perfect for them.
- Networking and asking others to share content with/for you – if you don't ask, they won't necessarily think to share *(NB by content I mean social media posts that you've created).*
- Raising your profile so that people get to know you, what you do, and what you offer, and more importantly, what you can do for them.

So, you now know that you could be doing more. Fabulous! Let's do this.

Step 1:

Go through the above "Leaving money on the table" list, and write a list of people that you could reach out to in each of the categories.

Step 2:

Reach out to those people, with a personalised message. Ask them how they are, and how their business is going. If you know you can help, invite them onto a call with you, and see where that call takes you. One of my clients brought in £6,000 additional income in the space of a few hours with this one exercise.

Part 3: Learn How to Give Back to Others Through Your Business

I'm incredibly lucky. I've never been homeless, and I can only imagine what it feels like not having the security of a home. With this in mind, it's long been an ambition of mine to help the homeless, and I spent some time mulling over ideas of how to use my business to support charity, before an incident occurred that accelerated this process.

The Universe Has a Funny Way of Helping You out

During an event where I was speaking, I met an incredible lady called Alisoun Mackenzie. Amongst other things, Alisoun helps businesses "give to profit". After speaking to her, I learned that she's written a book of that name, which teaches how you can add **cause marketing** to your business to support charities. I picked up a copy of the book, interested to see how it could improve my own practice. One of my long-term ambitions had been to coach/mentor 100 people for charity, but for some reason it had never felt like the right time. When I read Alisoun's book, I realised – I could coach/mentor 100 people as per my dream AND support a homeless charity at the same time. What a fabulous way to celebrate my then 5-year business birthday!

I felt excited about what I could create, and how I could help. I had a chat with Alisoun, who explained what I'd need to do to set it up, and that's how it all began. I decided to offer a £200 session for just £20, working with 100 people. I wanted to keep it easy, so that it would be manageable alongside running my online programme, and working with my 1:1 clients. So then, my next question was, who should I support? Luckily, Alisoun had that one covered too. I'm a bit of a caffeine addict, and well-known for it in my circles, where I get tagged in coffee posts and sent fun quotes! My husband and I were moving to Scotland, so she told me about a charity called Social Bite.

Social Bite have a chain of coffee shops in cities in Scotland, and are open to employing the homeless. 1 in 4 of their staff have struggled with homelessness, and customers can do a pay-it-forward coffee/meal. Plus, they're also working on setting up a village for the homeless, which is just incredible. They explain it better than I do. Check out the video on their website if you want to find out more. Coffee, Scotland, AND helping the homeless – I was so in! "Mission 100" was born! It was simple to set up (Check out Alisoun's book, *Give to Profit*, if you want to explore this in depth).

SOCIAL BITE | GOOD FOOD for a GOOD CAUSE

Here's a run through of what I did to get the project up and running:

Create a Sales Page

If it's just a quick offering like mine, then you don't need anything too fancy. It just needs to explain what you're doing and why. There are lots of great companies offering tools that you can use to create a simple sales page.

Link to Payment

Create a way for people to pay you. Again: KISS – Keep It Simple Sweetie, it doesn't need to be complicated.

Pull Together a Marketing Plan

Even though this is something you're doing for charity, like anything in business, you need to have a marketing plan in place. For my sessions, I shared the idea of what I wanted to achieve and then talked about it in lots of different places.

Here's a list of 7 things I included in my marketing plan. This will help you with other aspects of your business too:

1. Add a link at the bottom of your newsletters.
2. Share a link in your email signature.
3. Add a P.S. note to all your social media posts. (*P.S. I'm really excited to be helping (tag company) to help (your cause).*
4. Create a video explaining how it all works.
5. Create a single blog post about it, explaining what it is, and how/who you want to help. Share your story around why it's important to you, just like I have here.
6. Share a link to your post in any groups that you might be in.
7. Collect testimonials from your sessions and use them in your marketing.

In my "Mission 100" sessions I work with a little ladybird (you'll have to have a session to find out what I mean and help me raise money for Social Bite!) so after the session I send my clients a little image with a quote on. I ask for their permission to share their breakthrough message, and I also ask for a testimonial. This then creates two different images that I can share on social media.

Work out How Much You Want to Charge for Your Session

I started out at £20. Then, as time went on, I realised I wanted to charge more, so that I could raise more money for Social Bite. Now, I have the prices based on a rising scale.

Work out a Practical Budget

When promoting the interview, there will be costs involved, particularly when it comes to admin work. Be clear on what the costs are, and then you can explain in your marketing that a small percentage is retained to cover those costs.

Work out the Logistics of Fundraising for Your Chosen Charity

The charity for which you fundraise may have things in place to support you and/or guidelines you need to follow. It's always worth reaching out to the charity, to tell them what your initiative is and ask them if they have any resources to support your endeavour.

Talk to People About It

I'm sure by now you've figured out that I like to talk! When you're on calls, or out and about networking, tell people about what you're doing. Ask people to help you spread the word, so that you can raise more for your chosen charity.

Pay the Money as You Go

My circumstances changed as our big move to Scotland happened. We moved house twice, and lots of other big life things happened that prevented me from achieving my full goal of 100 people (yet). However, at the time of writing I've donated just over £400 to Social Bite, which is a lot better than just offering a cup of coffee to someone on the street. Am I giving up? Absolutely not! I will be continuing my "Mission 100", and I will reach that goal. It doesn't need to be a race. Sometimes life gets in the way. In fact, rather than giving up, I'm thinking of more ways that I can give back on a larger scale.

Note: If you mention in your marketing that you're donating a share of the sales price to charity, many countries (including the UK) have legislation on what you need to say and do. It's easy enough to comply with, just make sure you know what you're doing – which is why I work with Alisoun, who can help you with this too (www.givetoprofit.com).

Maybe You've Got an Idea That You Could Use to Support a Charity?

I like helping people, and I've often been known to give too much away because I like to help so much. By doing this, I can bring clients into my business, and it's a great way to give back too. It's so much fun knowing that your gifts and talents can provide someone with the support they need. Who knows, maybe there will be a "Mission 200" next, or something even bigger! I've got lots of ideas bubbling away!

If you are a business owner and would love to get an hour's worth of coaching/ mentoring support, while also helping the homeless, then check out this link – http://www.rubymcguire.com/mission-100. I'd love to support you. Even if it's not for you, maybe you know somebody that would love some business support. *(See what I did there!)*

Key Learnings:

That concludes my two pennies' worth of how to attract your "dreamie" clients. In our time together, you've learned:

- ✓ A Fear to Fabulousness strategy (a simple tool to help you move through fear).
- ✓ A model to help you create a visible and profitable business, including how to attract your "dreamie" clients with ease, and then how to keep them.
- ✓ How to give back as part of your business model.

I hope you've enjoyed our time together. If you want to find out more about working with me, either 1:1, in a group programme, or to experience a "Mission 100 session", come on over to my website at www.rubymcguire.com/work-with-me. I'd love to connect with you over a virtual cappuccino.

Biography

Ruby McGuire is a Business Mastery & Mindset Queen, and the author of Ruby's Visibility Tips. She shares super simple tips to master your business and mindset, to get your business noticed, so that you can attract "dreamie" clients. She lives in Scotland, is married to her soulmate, and is mum to three grown-up girls. Ruby is also the owner of a clever little dog – Lulu.

Ruby worked in HR for 11 years, with her last role being Head of HR. She has also worked as a trainer, and now runs a coaching/mentoring business. She does her best writing in local cafés, or at 5 am when it's pitch black with birds chirping outside. She loves to share with her readers how they can run a successful business AND have a life too!

You can reach Ruby here https://coach-accreditation.services/directories/find-an-accredited-coach-or-mentor/entry/219/

CHAPTER SEVEN

By

Monique Daigneault

4 Steps to Better Time Management

What Will I Learn?

- A time management system that will save at least two hours a day.
- How to implement a customer relations plan.
- Scalable technology, that saves valuable time.

Introduction

As you've worked your way through this precious gem of a book, you've worked hard on your mindset, goals, values, sales techniques, and a myriad of other critical strategies. Congratulations on your commitment and perseverance!

Discovering a livelihood that you are passionate about is a journey filled with excitement, fear, hesitation, and some of the highest highs you've ever experienced. Many of my clients tell me they've worked either for a boss or for themselves for decades, without recognising their true calling. So, if you're reading this book, you are well on your way to fulfilling your passion. For the last 30 years I've worked corporately, and I've also started four businesses – the first when I was only 25 years old and a single parent. As an executive coach, I work with senior leaders, CEOs, and business owners.

I know from my clients' experiences and from my own that to be successful in any endeavour, you need to be agile. To be agile you need to think quickly, shift gears rapidly, and access information without delay. Your clients depend on you to attend to their needs immediately, return calls promptly, and act as if they are your only priority.

Many of my clients try to keep critical information like dates, names, phone numbers, and tasks in their head, or even on sticky notes! You cannot do that – you MUST have a system in place. Being unorganised and unable to prioritise can impact your business strategy all the way from winning clients to keeping them. With each of my businesses, I found it critical to be organised, manage time properly, and service clients like they were the one and only! Your time is money, and if you don't leverage your time correctly, you will lose money by the hour. The good news is that you don't have to be born with great time management skills – they can be learned!

You have multiple priorities each day – administrative tasks, product development, projects, research, client contact, sales calls, and much more. As a matter of fact, some of your daily tasks will be things you've learned in this book. There will be days when you feel overwhelmed and feel like it's all too much to handle. That's ok, that's normal – and the next day will be better.

One way to ease your daily pressure is to have a good time management system in place. In this chapter you'll learn about a four-step system that I have used for decades. It includes getting organised, planning, managing time and tasks, and maintaining impeccable customer relations. When my clients use this system, they tell me they usually end up saving two hours a day! That adds up to a lot of time by month end. Don't be a slave to this system. Feel free to customise it to your liking and to your specific situation. No matter what line of work you're in, you can benefit from being more organised. I'll take you through an explanation of the system, along with a case study of Kathleen, an actual client who implemented it. Then, I will provide you with a check list of recommended hardware and software that, combined with the time management system, will help you with agility and scalability.

Case Study: Kathleen's Journey

Kathleen had over three decades of IT consulting experience, when she finally made the leap to start her own business. She was super excited, knew the IT world like the back of her hand, and already had two clients due to the many relationships she'd built over the years. Her initial goal was to make enough income to replace what she lost by quitting her corporate job. She ran the numbers and knew that in her first year she needed ten contracts, or ten clients, to meet her goal. She already had two, so she quickly began implementing techniques to bring in more clients.

Here was Kathleen's dilemma – in her corporate job she'd had a wonderful assistant, Anna. Anna magically handled everything: she reconciled all of Kathleen's travel expenses, scheduled her appointments, sent her reminders about upcoming commitments, answered minor client questions, organised her projects, responded to emails, made copies, prepared contracts, kept track of sales data, and even took care of computer issues. Anna was organised, efficient, reliable, an expert multi-tasker, and was exceptionally skilled when interfacing with clients. With Anna's help, Kathleen could focus specifically on the client and the consulting work. Everything else was handed off to Anna. But Kathleen no longer had Anna to rely upon, and certainly couldn't afford to hire that type of help.

Within the first month of launching her new consulting business, Kathleen was completely overwhelmed. She could barely keep up with servicing her two clients because of all the other work. She was trying to network, work with her mentor, schedule sales calls, return calls and emails, get her software up and running, develop contract templates, and hand off financial responsibilities to the accountant. Within that first month, Kathleen received scathing emails from two leads in her sales funnel. They each told her that they had left multiple messages for her, wanting to learn more about her services, but they never received a call back – so they decided to take their business elsewhere. Kathleen was devastated! She didn't even recall the messages, much less how she'd handled them. She wondered if she had lost the numbers, accidentally deleted them, or just forgot to return the calls.

Kathleen had also committed to writing an article for a very prestigious consulting magazine. She thought it was a great idea, because she loved to write, and it was part of her marketing strategy. However, she missed the deadline, so the editor chose another writer.

Kathleen also dropped the ball with one of her current clients. That client wanted Kathleen to come on site in 10 days, to oversee a software implementation. They needed a response to their email request within 24 hours, so that they could obtain her security clearance. Kathleen didn't open the email until two days later. As a result, she had to oversee the implementation remotely, and the client was not happy. After only one month in business, Kathleen was exhausted and failing miserably. At this rate, how could she possibly take on eight more clients?

Step 1: Getting Organised

The first place to begin is to organise your environment. If you don't have an "environment" then you need to create one, especially if you work from home. Working from your kitchen table is not effective or efficient. The numerous distractions and interruptions will make it impossible for you to focus and concentrate. So, find a space that is private and large enough for a desk, chair, filing cabinet, and possibly a bookshelf. Depending on your situation, you may be using your computer's video camera for conference calls. With that in mind, be mindful of what is behind your chair, because it will show up on camera. If necessary, have a decorative room divider or a backdrop that can be put up when you're on camera. Position the furniture to leverage space, natural lighting, and proximity to often-used items. Plan to always keep your office space decluttered, so that you can find things quickly, and so that things don't accidentally get thrown away.

Getting organised isn't just about your physical space. Think about your paper files, your electronic files, manuals, and have a plan to back things up in case of loss. I have one two-drawer file cabinet that gets purged every six months. Many people keep buying bigger and bigger file cabinets, yet never clean out the one they have. Once they do, it becomes obvious that the original one was all that was needed. Don't just think about your current needs. Think ahead about what size file cabinet you might need in the future. Purchase that, declutter it routinely, and you'll never need another one!

You **will** need a filing system. This should consist of hanging files, the file folders that go inside, and labels. My system is alphabetical, and all folders are labelled based on the client or project. If you also have a bookcase, apply the same system to all books and manuals on the shelves. Typically, an alphabetical system allows you to locate things quickly, and they should be put back the same way.

You will also have electronic files and emails, which should follow the exact same filing system. On your hard drive, try to have electronic folders and files that are labelled the same way as those in your file cabinet. For example, in your file cabinet, if you have a hanging file labelled *Project One* and inside that is a file folder labelled *Advertising,* then your electronic folders and files should follow suit. The reason for this is that for every client, you will likely have both hard copy and electronic versions of the same file/contract. You need to make sure they get filed in similar ways throughout the engagement.

The same is true for email folders. Create email folders, and sub folders, for each client or project, and try to keep the labelling consistent with the hard copy and electronic files. Be sure to save important emails to these folders, just in case you need to refer to them later. Many times, I copy myself in on emails and then just file the latest version. Like your paper and electronic files, emails also need to be purged. I clean out my email folders at mid-year and year end.

It is critical to have an external hard drive to back up all your electronic files. The last thing you want to deal with is a system failure, a theft, or an accidental deletion of files that prevents you from accessing crucial information. I back up my files weekly, but you'll need to use your judgement here. At a minimum, you'll want to do a system back-up on a monthly basis.

Getting organised takes discipline and consistency, but it's better to put in the time up front, than trying to do business in a cluttered, unorganised environment.

Let's see how Kathleen handled Step 1.

Case Study: How Kathleen Got Organised

Kathleen was working from home and, although she wasn't working from her kitchen table, she was sharing an office with her husband. He wasn't in the office much of the time, but Kathleen was still distracted by sharing a space with him. Fortunately, they had a second room that was unoccupied, and it was perfect for Kathleen. She used her creativity to turn it into a cosy, professional office, with a corner desk to maximise space. Adding a bookcase and file cabinet gave her enough room for training manuals and client files. She had been sharing a file cabinet with her husband, so having one all to herself felt better. Video calls were common in her line of work, so she purchased a trifold room divider, that she could place behind her chair for a professional background. When not in use, it could be folded and stored.

The filing system was the hardest for Kathleen, because she was not used to putting things away – which contributed to her problems. She started with the bookcase, and alphabetised all her books and manuals.

To organise her filing cabinet, Kathleen labelled three hanging folders, and hung them in alphabetical order: *Client A, Client B, Operations*. In the *Client A* hanging file she added three alphabetised folders labelled: *Contract Info, Implementation, Post Implementation*. These folders would contain anything related to these three topics. If the project grew, she would add more folders. If she took on more clients, she would duplicate the overall process with new folders. Kathleen labelled the folders in the same way for *Client B*. The *Operations* hanging folder contained four alphabetised folders labelled: *Banking, Business Plan, Receipts,* and *Solopreneur Training Programmes*. That was all that was in her two-drawer filing cabinet, but she knew it would fill quickly as her business grew. She made a note to review the contents every six months, and purge anything she no longer needed. Having an organised environment gave Kathleen a good feeling, but she knew it would take discipline to maintain the new process.

Kathleen then moved on to her electronic and email files. She set up electronic folders and files, email folders, and sub folders, and labelled everything the same as in her file cabinet. In Kathleen's line of work, she received mainly electronic information. Instinctively, she knew that she may need to expand her electronic filing system beyond what was in her file cabinet. But she was okay with that, because she was learning to customise the system. Again, she made a note to review and purge her electronic files every six months.

> There was a lot of sensitive and confidential information on Kathleen's computer hard drive. So, she purchased a small external drive to back up her electronic files. She made a note to do a backup each Friday night, before leaving her office for the weekend.
>
> Kathleen stated: 'Getting organised took a bit of effort, especially moving into the new office and getting it set up. But I felt very good after completing this step. I felt like there might be hope for overcoming my issues from the previous month.'

Step 2: Planning

Many people tell me that they don't have time to plan their day, because they have too much to do. In response, I tell them that planning is the solution to having too much to do! My clients who use this time management system report that they save a minimum of two hours each day. It's true – investing just 10-12 minutes in planning your day will save at least two hours of wasted time and effort every day! Multiply two hours by your hourly rate, and that is the money you're saving daily, by making time to plan. So, how can you NOT plan?

When you plan effectively, you are essentially taking control of your day, rather than letting the day take control of you! You take control by committing only to tasks and initiatives that are in alignment with your goals, setting boundaries, and eliminating procrastination. Let's take these one at a time.

You've already learned that setting goals is a critical activity. Once you set goals, you must focus on them daily, by breaking them down into actionable steps and tasks. You need to spend time each day taking steps toward these goals. There are two mistakes my clients make when working on their goals. The first mistake is that they fail to work on their goals each day. In **Step 3: Managing Time and Tasks** you will read about how to schedule daily time for this, so that you can achieve small steps on a continual basis.

The second mistake my clients make is to commit to things that do not align with their goals, or even their values for that matter. This sucks up their time, energy, and resources, without any return on investment. In the future, before you take on any request, anything that sounds cool, or even something that sounds fun, do the following exercise.

Exercise #1: Align Action with Values and Goals

Think about your **current** daily actions and write your answers to the questions below.

1. Do they align with my values, or are they in conflict?
2. How do they align with my strategic goals?
3. What will be the return on investment (in time, money, satisfaction, relationship building)?

Setting time boundaries is an important part of the planning mindset, and it ties into the exercise you have completed. If something comes your way that does not tie in with your goals, you need to start saying 'NO' or 'Not at this time'. Some examples of people, or time vampires, crossing your time boundaries are:

- A friend who calls excessively during your workday to vent about her personal life.
- Clients who routinely run late for meetings or cancel at the last minute.
- People who don't respond to you, causing you to constantly follow up with them.
- Clients who pay late, causing you to have to chase them down for payment.
- Requests from others to take on additional projects or volunteer work when those things aren't part of your goals.

If these things are happening to you on a regular basis, you need to learn to say 'NO', which is easier said than done. As you read further, you will see just how Kathleen handled her time vampires. She even realised ways that she, herself, was wasting time. When you set time boundaries – by saying 'NO' – you will make realistic commitments, prioritise easier, stay focused longer, and manage interruptions with ease. You will get more done in less time, leaving you with MORE time to handle other pressing matters – like working with your clients.

Exercise #2: Setting Boundaries

Ask yourself the following questions, and then write down your responses:

1. Who are my time vampires?
2. In what ways do I waste my own time during the day?
3. What are some ways I can set boundaries with myself and others?

Let's talk about procrastination. Now, there may indeed be some deep-seated behaviours related to this habit. However, what is often labelled "procrastination" is simply something that stems from being overwhelmed. When trying to juggle multiple priorities without a good time management system, it's easy to become overwhelmed. As you get overwhelmed, tasks build up, and nothing gets done because you don't know where to start. Once there is a system in place, something to keep you on track, you'll feel more in control and start seeing measurable results – just like Kathleen did! We'll look at all her results after step four, but for now let's see how she implemented this step.

Case Study: How Kathleen Implemented Planning

Kathleen thought about her goals for the first year of her business. She listed them and then added tasks under each main goal. There were only three, but she felt very overwhelmed just looking at them! Here was her list:

1. Bring on eight new clients
    a. Network for new target clients.
    b. Market the business (advertising, writing, speaking).
    c. Write proposals/contracts.
    d. Conduct sales meetings.
    e. Possible travel.
    f. Administrative duties (emails, schedule meetings, website/LinkedIn updates).
2. Complete certification training
    a. Research training.
    b. Complete training.

3. Manage business budget

    a. Meet with the accountant.

    b. File and track receipts.

    c. Review budget at least monthly.

Once Kathleen looked at her goals, she realised two things: 1. She was NOT working on them daily, and 2. She was doing a lot of "other" things that **weren't** on her list. Then she listed out those "other" things, and here is what she came up with:

- Chatting with friends on the phone during the day.
- Turning on the TV during the day to watch the afternoon news.
- Tracking down one of her clients on a regular basis when they missed an appointment.
- Spending a lot of time collecting late payments from the previous client.
- Marketing to and networking with people who were not her ideal clients.
- Running errands in the middle of the day, getting her hair done, shopping.
- Helping a local organisation arrange a Pet Adoption campaign.

This is what Kathleen told me: 'When I actually listed out my goals, then listed out what I was doing each day, I saw the huge gap! It suddenly became clear that I was not leveraging my time or managing it well.'

Basically, Kathleen was treating her business as a hobby, by not establishing set work hours and allowing herself to be distracted by things unrelated to her goals. One of the best perks of being a solopreneur is that you have a flexible schedule. However, you must be disciplined, and you must be experiencing tangible results. You cannot whittle away your billable hours by watching TV.

As part of the planning process, Kathleen needed to eliminate time wasters and time vampires, and become more disciplined. Here are some things that she did to close that gap:

- Told friends she could no longer talk on the phone during her work day. If they called anyway, she simply did not answer.
- Stopped leaving during the day to run errands, and stopped watching the news.

- Ceased work on the Pet Adoption campaign, and let the organisation know that she **might** be able to help in the next year **if** she had time.
- Set boundaries with clients regarding late payments and missed appointments.
- Changed her marketing and networking strategy so that her time was spent wisely.

Kathleen then tackled her habit of procrastination; she had a few interesting insights. Firstly, she learned that she was most definitely procrastinating because of feeling overwhelmed. As much as she wanted to be a solopreneur, she just was not prepared for all there was to do. As things built up, she didn't know what to handle first. Secondly, she realised that some things she purposely put off because she just didn't want to do them. Certain things did not bring her the same type of joy she felt when working directly with her clients. Those joyless tasks were related to administrative and budgeting items.

I coached Kathleen around her second insight, to help her break down the roadblock, and she came to an agreement with herself. She committed to doing the joyless work, daily – without putting it off – knowing that eventually she would get more clients and build up her revenue. She promised herself that as soon as she could afford to, she would hire an assistant. So, those joyless tasks became her incentive. By doing them, she would be spending her time wisely, which would ultimately bring in new clients. With more revenue, she could hire someone to do those tasks. It was a shift in perspective, and a shift in mindset, but one she was willing to try.

Kathleen later told me in a coaching session, 'Moving through this step was eye opening for me! It seemed too simple to be successful, and I couldn't believe how hard I was making everything, and how hard I was being on myself.'

Step 3: Managing Time and Tasks

In **Step 2: Planning**, you read about the importance of breaking down your goals into actionable steps and tasks. I'm presuming you identified your goals in the previous chapters. Before getting started on **Step 3**, please complete the exercise below to break down your goals into tasks. This is a critical exercise to complete before you can learn how to carve out time to work on them daily.

Exercise #3: Breaking Down Goals into Tasks

In the previous case study, you saw how Kathleen listed her goals for the year. Under each goal she listed the tasks associated with that goal. You'll need to break down your goals the same way in this exercise. Follow the template below, and if you have more than four goals and tasks feel free to customise the template.

1. Goal #1
    a. Task
    b. Task
    c. Task
    d. Task
2. Goal #2
    a. Task
    b. Task
    c. Task
    d. Task
3. Goal #3
    a. Task
    b. Task
    c. Task
4. Goal #4
    a. Task
    b. Task
    c. Task
    d. Task

These goals and tasks will become your daily, weekly, and monthly focus for the year. Now, you may have a few additional miscellaneous items to handle periodically but, for the most part, this where you will put your time and energy.

Managing your time and tasks must be done strategically and systematically for the best results. You will use two tools for this – the calendar and the task list, which are both located in most email programmes. The sophistication of the task list will vary depending on your email system. However, if you don't like what you have, there are several highly sophisticated task list programmes independent from your email programme.

Exercise #4: Choose Your Task List

Read this article to see descriptions and screenshots of various tasks lists: https://blog.hubspot.com/marketing/best-to-do-list-apps-tools

Open your email programme, and locate the Task Tab and the Calendar Tab. Many people are familiar with the Calendar Tab, but most don't even realise that the Task Tab exists within their email program. Make sure you can find both. If you don't like the task list that you see, then choose an application from the article you just read. Whatever you choose, be sure that it is accessible from your computer **and** your phone.

Note: Some people choose to use Word or Excel to track their daily tasks. These typically are not efficient ways to track time sensitive goals and tasks, so I encourage you to explore the options given in the activity.

Exercise #5: List Your Goals and Sub-Tasks

In your chosen task list application, list your main goals and their sub-tasks. There may also be an area where you can list deadline dates. If so, it's important for you to do this. Deadline dates will keep you on track. Maybe all your goals are due by the end of the year, but your tasks will need to be done earlier, in order to meet your year-end deadlines. Configure your task list to include all this information. If there is a way to prioritise each goal and/or task, do so. Again, this will force you to analyse what's important so that you can leverage your time and work smarter.

Note: If you have trouble prioritising your goals and tasks, take this advice. Your priority should be the tasks that are directly related to making money. For example, if you have two tasks, taking a networking call and completing a client proposal, the client proposal takes priority! Money-making tasks come first.

Once you've listed and prioritised your tasks, go to your calendar and start **Time Blocking**. Time blocking is when you set up a meeting with yourself to work on things from your task list. Time blocking ensures two things:

1. You have daily, focused, uninterrupted time.
2. You are working on your goals daily.

This is where discipline and boundaries come into play. You must have time vampires under control, a consistent work schedule in place, be able to manage interruptions, and have a commitment to not waste your own time. If you don't, this system will not work for you, and you'll be back to square one! I recommend that you time block for one month at a time, and then adjust and reprioritise weekly and even daily if you must. Here's how this works:

Exercise #6: Time Blocking

In your calendar, schedule all appointments that you know about for the upcoming month – personal appointments, business appointments, networking meetings, etc. **Do this at the end of each month for the upcoming month.**

Then, look at your task list and try to estimate how much time you can spend throughout the month on the tasks from each goal. Ideally, you'll want to make time **daily** for each goal's tasks. Once you've identified the estimated time, go back to your calendar and block out that time so that it shows up as a meeting with yourself.

For example, maybe you estimate that you can spend one hour a day (Monday through Friday, all month long) on goal #3 tasks, from 2-3 pm. If that is realistic to you, then set that up in your calendar as a meeting with yourself.

But maybe goal #2 is a higher priority and you want to spend two hours every day on it (Monday through Friday, all month long). You see that you have some open time from 9-11 am each day. If that works for you then set that up in your calendar.

However, goal #1 takes a lot of focus, and you'd rather spend four hours on it at one time, and you can't do that every day. You see, though, that you can do that every **Thursday** from 9-1 pm for the month. If that's what works for you, then set it up like that. The point here is that you are being disciplined but also flexible and realistic.

It is reasonable to assume that your nicely scheduled, time blocked, month will shift weekly, maybe even daily as the month goes on. This is to be expected, and that's the reason for the next exercise.

Exercise #7: Plan and Shift Your Week

At the end of each week (preferably Friday), look ahead to the upcoming week and fine tune or revise your calendar, task list, and time blocking for that week. Maybe on Monday of the following week you have a 9 am networking meeting and cannot spend from 9-11 am working on goal #2 tasks. So, you may need to shift goal #2 tasks to later in the day, or double up on it later in the week. Or maybe you decide to cancel it altogether. That's okay, because you'll still be working on it Tuesday through Friday of that week. This system is designed to be a guideline for you, keep you disciplined, and keep your goals in front of you daily. But you don't have to become a slave to it. There are many ways to customise the system so that it can work for you.

Now that you've learned how to plan and shift your week in advance, the next exercise will show you how to look ahead to the **next day** and shift your schedule as needed.

Exercise #8: Plan and Shift Your Day

At the end of each day, look ahead to the following day, and fine tune or revise your calendar, task list, and time blocking for that day. This is like what you did in **Exercise #7**, except now you are only looking ahead to the following day. Perhaps nothing needs to change for the next day, but make it a habit to check anyway. When you see what's coming up, you then need to plan for it. For example, if you have an in-person or virtual meeting, make sure to prepare the night before. Gather notes, directions, phone numbers, and key agenda items so that you are fully prepared. One additional step I perform before meeting with anyone is to research them briefly on LinkedIn, as a reminder of their position, background, and location. This takes less than 10 minutes!

I mentioned earlier that you might have miscellaneous tasks coming up daily that aren't part of your main goals and tasks. That's ok, but time block those too! My suggestion is to do "like activities" at the same time to stay efficient. We call this "chunking" your time. For example, on Monday you are working diligently on your time blocked tasks, and Client #1 emails you asking for a contract change and a phone call, that same day. Then, Client #2 sends a detailed email that you must review and respond to, that same day. Chunk your time by doing everything for one client, and then move on to the other client, whomever you deem a higher priority. By chunking, you are not splitting your focus by jumping back and forth between client requests. Splitting your focus can waste valuable time.

Managing your time and tasks on a monthly, weekly, and daily basis keeps you agile and focused on your goals. It also keeps you in the mindset of accomplishing things daily. You already learned about the importance of mindset in an earlier chapter. This step of managing time and tasks was the hardest for Kathleen. Let's see how she handled it.

Case Study: How Kathleen Managed Time and Tasks

If you recall, when Kathleen implemented **Step 2: Planning** she listed her goals as such:

1. Bring on eight new clients
    a. Network for new target clients.
    b. Market the business (advertising, writing, speaking).
    c. Write proposals/contracts.
    d. Conduct sales meetings.
    e. Possible travel.
    f. Administrative duties (emails, schedule meetings, website/LinkedIn updates).
2. Complete certification training
    a. Research training.
    b. Complete training.
3. Manage business budget
    a. Meet with the accountant.
    b. File and track receipts.
    c. Review budget at least monthly.

Kathleen had never used a task list before, but her email programme had one that she really liked, so she chose that. Within the task list she labelled the first line with her first goal – "Bring on eight new clients". On subsequent, indented lines she listed each related task from a-f. She did the same thing for her second and third goals, and their tasks. The only difference was that some tasks had deadline dates, so she listed those dates next to the tasks. This is how it looked:

Complete certification training

- Research training – **30 September**.
- Complete training – **30 November**.

Manage business budget

- Meet with the accountant – **15 September**.
- File and track receipts.
- Review budget at least monthly.

Notice that these are deadline dates – the date that the task must be completed, not start dates. Some people work best if they give themselves a start date and a deadline date. That's fine, and it's one example of how the system can be modified. Create your task list the way you see fit, providing you follow it!

Once Kathleen entered her goals, tasks, and deadlines into her task list, she felt a sense of relief. She said, 'I never really created this type of visual before especially with deadline dates. No wonder I always felt like I was randomly floundering every day and not really accomplishing anything.'

Kathleen then went on to time block the month of September. Now, daily, it was typical for her to have phone calls and emails to respond to. This seemed to be one of her downfalls, and caused abrasion with clients, because she wasn't responding fast enough. Kathleen set a standard to respond to them within one business day. So, she blocked out the first hour of her day, Monday through Friday, to return phone calls and emails. She knew that it might take more than an hour and, if so, she would extend it. But, for the time being, she dedicated from 9-10 am to that task.

Kathleen went on to time block the rest of her tasks: 1 hour per day for networking, one hour a day to work on marketing, two hours per day for writing proposals, one hour per day for miscellaneous administrative tasks, etc. She would be reviewing the budget only at month end, so she blocked out four hours for this task on the last day of the month. She also factored in doctor appointments, a meeting with her accountant, and time for research training throughout the month. This training research was not daily, but she estimated that it would take three hours to complete, so she scheduled it to take place for one hour, for three days in September. That way it would be completed by her deadline date.

The first week of Kathleen's time blocking felt strange, and she found it hard to stick to. Sometimes she veered off course, but when that happened she just reminded herself to follow her calendar. At the end of her first week, she looked ahead to the following week. She had made a last-minute doctor's appointment on Wednesday, that would interfere with her hour of marketing activities. But she noticed that on Tuesday she had a one hour opening, so she moved Wednesday's marketing activities to Tuesday. This meant that on Tuesday she would be working on marketing activities for two hours, rather than the usual one hour. This adjustment worked well for her, because she had received another writing opportunity, and writing was part of her marketing strategy. So, this would give her two full hours on Tuesday to focus on her writing project. She made similar adjustments for the upcoming week, and by Monday of that week she felt organised. Then, at the end of each day that week, Kathleen practised planning ahead for the following day.

At the end of the day on Monday, she found that there was nothing to adjust for Tuesday. She did have two online meetings to attend, and she needed to prepare for them. Kathleen spent 10 minutes getting organised for those meetings, and even had time to send reminder emails to the other attendees. By Tuesday, everything flowed just like clockwork!

This was Kathleen's routine for the month of September. By month end she had logged 20 hours of networking, 20 hours of marketing, 40 hours on proposals and contracts, completed her training research, and reviewed the budget. She had spent time on her other tasks also, and was able to keep up with emails and phone messages. Kathleen was starting to get the hang of the system, and she felt like things were finally getting done!

You now have a better idea about managing your time and tasks. I want to emphasise once again how important it is that you do this in a way that works for you. My clients tweak this four-step process, especially the third step, based on their business model and business needs. It is also important to understand that this is not about killing yourself to knock out your goals each week. Flexibility and agility are about adjusting and shifting course as you go. This system promotes awareness and consistency to help you stay on track. The process will make a massive difference in how much you can achieve.

Step 4: Impeccable Customer Relations

The fourth step in this system will help you manage your clients and keep them happy. You've already seen a glimpse of that in the previous steps, especially when Kathleen allotted one hour each morning to respond to phone calls and emails.

However, there is more to client relations than just responding. An organised businessperson will track clients and contacts in a Customer Relationship Management

(CRM) database. There are numerous platforms available, and you will have to research what is best for you. Be sure to choose one that is scalable, one that handles more data as your business grows, or one that you can upgrade. Many CRM programs allow you to track the status of proposals, the amount of revenue from clients, notes after meetings, and which clients are past due. All of this simplifies your life and keeps you agile. The last thing you want to be doing is digging around in paperwork, trying to locate data. In addition, many CRM programmes automatically come with an integrated task list. I use the task list in my email programme rather than the one in my CRM.

After you implement your CRM, you must then make time to access, review, and update it regularly. It becomes part of your daily or weekly tasks, and gets time blocked into your calendar just like everything else. Most likely, you'll only need to time block fifteen minutes a day for this task. Examples of CRM updates might include notes from phone calls with clients or vendors, reminders of who to follow up with, or adding a new prospect.

Exercise #9: Research and Implement Your CRM

Research, implement and time block your CRM into your calendar.

Once you have a CRM to keep your client data organised, you then need to set standards to deliver exceptional customer service. Make time for your clients and be proactive, it will save you time down the road. It is much cheaper to keep a current client happy than to find a new client to replace an unhappy one. Setting standards is a proactive way of thoroughly servicing clients through the entire lifecycle of an engagement. Here are some examples of standards:

- Return phone calls and emails within a specified time frame, for example one business day.
- Check in on clients or ask for feedback within a specified time frame, for example monthly.
- Send a gift to clients on their birthday or anniversary (these dates can be tracked in your CRM).
- Talk to clients in advance and identify potential risks that could occur. Put a mitigation plan in place.

- Complete a deliverable earlier than promised.
- Provide an extra service without charging for it.
- Ask clients how best to communicate with them (email, phone, text, meetings, status reports) so that you are accommodating **their** needs, not yours. This becomes your communication plan.
- Contact clients ASAP if something looks like it'll become a problem (don't wait until it does become a problem).
- Make client problems the top priority in your day, until they are resolved.
- Throughout the engagement, listen for other problems and offer additional solutions, services, or products to assist them.
- When you are ready to finish up with a client, send a feedback survey.
- Ask for testimonials that will include their name and business to help them advertise.
- Send referrals to your clients (and ask them for referrals); this is part of relationship building.
- Depending on the type of business you have, don't charge hourly! If possible, charge by the package, the project, the job, or offer something all-inclusive. You are selling solutions, not hours.

These standards become your Customer Relations Plan (CRP). You will need to time block this. Yes, you need to factor in time to make your clients happy. Relationships do not evolve without a lot of attention.

Exercise #10: Create a Customer Relations Plan (CRP)

Create a CRP by making a list of standards. Use what you like from the previous examples and then add your own. When finished, determine which ones can be grouped into a segment of time, and time block them into your calendar. You may not need to time block your CRP daily, but at a minimum it should be monthly.

If you recall, Kathleen had two very upset clients. They were happier once she time blocked an hour every morning to respond to their emails and phone calls. However, Kathleen knew she still needed to do more, so she implemented a CRM and created a CRP.

Case Study: Kathleen's CRM and CRP

After being coached on this step, Kathleen said, 'Step four confused me until I got clear that I had to time block my CRM **and** my CRP! These are different; one is the software tool and the other is the process directly related to keeping my clients happy. Once I got my head around this it was easy!'

Kathleen chose her CRM software, set it up, and then blocked out time daily to access and update it. That's the part that kept her client information organised. An updated CRM is a big part of delivering impeccable customer relations – it's the piece that works behind the scenes.

Then Kathleen developed her CRP, a list of 20 standards that really branded her business. She was very proud of these standards, and made a point to include them in her marketing material. She realised that having a list does no good unless you implement it! So, she looked over the list and determined what things needed to be time blocked into her calendar. For example, one of her standards was to send a birthday/anniversary message to clients. She decided that at the end of every month she would do a "sort" in her CRM, to see which clients had birthdays and anniversaries in the upcoming month. She would then send them a special message. She estimated that it would take about one hour each month to do the "sort" and send the messages. So, she time blocked one hour on the last day of each month to do this.

Another example, was that Kathleen wanted to ask for feedback from clients on a regular basis, so that she could improve her services. Her contracts usually lasted about 12 months, so she decided to ask for feedback every three months. She wanted to do this by telephone. Assuming she'd have 10 clients as planned, she estimated about a 30-minute call per client, five hours in total for these conversations. She then went to her calendar and time blocked five hours during the last week of every third month, one hour a day during those weeks.

Kathleen realised that not every standard needed to be time blocked. For example, she decided to change her method of bidding on projects from an hourly rate, to a project rate. This was a standard she knew her clients would like, but it didn't need to be time blocked. Instead, she added it to her proposal template, so that when she wrote up a proposal she could just fill in the field.

Kathleen went through her entire list of standards and either time blocked them or implemented them in some other way. 'I realised that developing impeccable customer relations is also a state of mind,' said Kathleen, 'not just software or a process. It's a way of thinking and remembering to treat your clients like gold every day. A mindset can't be time blocked but the time blocking certainly helped me develop the mindset!'

Kathleen's Overall Results

Kathleen's biggest goal for her first year in business was to obtain eight new clients and hang on to the first two clients. By applying this 4-step time management system, she achieved the following results in her first year:

- Added 200 new prospects to her CRM database via successful weekly networking.
- Wrote and launched a new book, which increased her revenue by 25 percent.
- Completed a highly coveted certification training. which placed her in the top 2 percent of consultants across the country.
- Routinely completed proposals two days earlier than planned.
- Completed client engagements an average of two weeks early and 10 percent under budget.
- Became known in the industry for her high standards (CRP).
- Received 15 referrals from happy clients.
- Hired an administrative assistant to handle admin duties and the automation of her business.
- Obtained **11 new clients** in her first year, while still maintaining her two original clients.

Exercise #11: Choose Your Technology

The following exercise is designed to help you think about what technology is needed for your business model. To be scalable and agile, you must automate as much as possible, so think about that when you complete the exercise. You can customise the list based on your business model. When purchasing technology, the idea is to plan for growth.

In the left-hand column, tick what you will need to purchase and implement to make your business activities scalable, organised, and efficient. Add to the list if necessary.

Tick	Technology for Agility	Comments
	New/faster computer	
	Email programme	Be sure this can also be accessed from your phone.
	Calendar and task list	Be sure this can also be accessed from your phone.
	External hard drive	Schedule data backups weekly.
	Customer Relationship Management (CRM) software	
	Video conferencing software	For example, Skype or Zoom.
	E-fax program	This is a fax program that is linked to your email, so that you don't need a fax machine.
	Microphone	Important for recording or delivering webinars.
	Handsfree ear piece	
	Scanner, printer, fax, copier	
	Virus protection	
	Portable phone charger	
	Client scheduling software	Needed only if you want your clients to schedule their own appointments, rather than going through you for scheduling.
	Website	Websites can be automated with documents, enrolment forms, contracts, and surveys, so that you don't have to handle these administrative tasks.
	A service contract for computer repairs	This saves hours each month, because if you have a computer problem then the technician can remote into your computer and fix it, eliminating many headaches for you.

You are busy, and you want to save time without sacrificing the quality of your product or service. So, get ahead of the competition and implement a streamlined time management system that allows you to be agile, organised, and efficient. If you are not used to managing your time, then this four-step system will certainly take you out of your comfort zone. Hopefully, you implemented each step along the way in this chapter. If you didn't, then take a risk, step out of your comfort zone, and get started.

Remember, you'll save approximately two hours a day by implementing this system. You will end up bringing on clients faster and keeping them longer. The bottom line is that you will have more billable hours available! I use this system, and so do my clients. I have also implemented all the technology on the check list from **Exercise #11**.

Kathleen is living, breathing proof that this system works. Her results were almost unheard of, and considering the way she started off, there is no way she could have achieved those results without this system. One of the many benefits of this system is that it's customisable. It's based on your business model, your goals, your calendar availability, and your priorities. If you already have a great work space, then skip step one. If you already have a CRM but no CRP, then implement only the CRP portion. Maybe you already do a version of time blocking that works well for you. If so, great! See if it needs tweaking and move on to the next step. It's totally up to you; you can fall back on this system whenever you need to. It's another tool in your toolbox, and one that will keep you agile and ahead of the competition.

If you're still feeling like this is a bit out of your comfort zone, don't worry. You don't have to implement this system alone! I'm going to list my contact information on the next page, and I want you to contact me if you need to be coached through this. We'll schedule a breakthrough call to see what you need, and decide if we'll work well together. If not, that's fine too; you'll still get some great value from our first call. Congratulations to you, for being well on your way to better time management!

Key Action Points:

- ✓ Organise your environment.
- ✓ Create a customised filing system.
- ✓ Set time boundaries.
- ✓ Break down goals into actionable steps.
- ✓ Create a prioritised task list.
- ✓ Time block your task list monthly, weekly, and daily.
- ✓ Implement a CRM.
- ✓ Develop a Customer Relations Plan (CRP).
- ✓ Identify and implement scalable technology.

Biography

Monique Daigneault, founder of MD Consulting, is a seasoned Executive Coach, author, and dynamic facilitator with over three decades of corporate and entrepreneurial experience. Monique has the unique ability to build immediate trust and quickly align clients with their true values and desired direction. Her clients benefit from practical and behavioural changes that are sustainable and measurable, as well as business strategies that enhance success. As a lifelong learner, Monique has achieved seven industry specific certifications, a Bachelor of Science in Management, and a Master of Science in Industrial/Organisational Psychology. Monique is from the United States and spends 25% of her time volunteering in Europe and China.

You can get in touch with Monica via www.executiveinfluence.coach.

Summary

Congratulations for your commitment and dedication to reading this business handbook. Your journey so far has encompassed many elements.

Firstly, Adele introduced you to the importance of authenticity, values, and trust when dealing with clients. You were then encouraged by Lorna to look at how applying your spiritual principles will help you to deliver your mission of helping others. This was followed by Ali, who asked you to consider the importance of mindset as well as addressing motivation, dealing with fear, failure and rejection, and standing out from the crowd.

At the mid-way point you were encouraged by Anna to consider the emotional elements of running a successful business, and to clarify and reaffirm what is important to you in being successful. Maria then invited you to explore, through her P.A.V.E model, how creating powerful, authentic, and valued relationships will contribute enormously to your success.

In the penultimate chapter, Ruby provided you with three strategies to create your dream business, including the five steps that you need to follow in order to be visible and profitable. And finally, Monique presented you with a time management system that will save you valuable time each day, as well as information on how to implement a customer relations plan, and information on useful technology.

And there you have it – a fully-fledged action plan to help you succeed in your business. However, just reading a book does not make you successful. A key theme for every chapter is the need to act, to do something tangible for your business. The tips, exercises, and challenges are there to help you grow, but you must act. After all, there's no impact to doing nothing. This book is the first step in your journey, so take action today, and make the lessons count.

Idea

10%
achieved

Idea + decision

40%
achieved

Idea + decision + plan of action

50%
achieved

Idea + decision + plan of action + tell someone

65%
achieved

Idea + decision + plan of action + tell someone and report back results

90%
achieved

As you read earlier, when we have an idea we're 10% likely to achieve it. My idea was to create a platform for members to raise their profile by reaching a wider audience.

Building on the momentum of my idea, I made a decision, and I created a plan of action. Then I went public, with overwhelming results.

After whittling the response down to these magnificent 7 co-authors, I was 90% more likely to succeed. And we did, because here we are. You've read our uniquely entrepreneurial book that speaks to wannabe solopreneurs and the many business owners who've reached a plateau.

These magnificent 7 co-authors have shared their successes and lessons learnt; they've offered you motivation, guidance, strategies, tips, techniques, tools and a host of practical exercises designed to gently challenge you and your business to succeed.

In "The Shawshank Redemption", Andy Dufresne leaves a letter for his friend Ellis Boyd "Red" Redding. Part of the letter reads *"...And if you've come this far, maybe you're willing to come a little further.*"

You have come this far, dear reader. How much further are you willing to go to succeed in your business? It's up to you!

Dawn Campbell, IAPC&M

Free e-Guides available here https://coach-accreditation.services/directories/

https://coach-accreditation.services/accreditation/membership-benefits/

For more information about accreditation contact us here

https://coach-accreditation.services/contact/

30041323R00106

Printed in Great
Britain
by Amazon